NEEDS ASSESSMENT
A USER'S GUIDE

NEEDS ASSESSMENT

A USER'S GUIDE

Roger Kaufman
Alicia M. Rojas
Hanna Mayer

EDUCATIONAL TECHNOLOGY PUBLICATIONS
ENGLEWOOD CLIFFS, NEW JERSEY 07632

Library of Congress Cataloging-in-Publication Data

Kaufman, Roger A.
    Needs assessment : a user's guide / Roger Kaufman, Alicia M. Rojas, Hanna Mayer.
      p.   cm.
    Includes bibliographical references and index.
    ISBN 0-87778-258-X
    1. Strategic planning.   2. Needs assessment.   I. Rojas, Alicia Mabel. II. Mayer, Hanna.
HD30.28.K378   1993
823'.8099287--dc20   92-45188
                                                               CIP

Copyright © 1993 Educational Technology Publications, Inc., Englewood Cliffs, New Jersey 07632.

All rights reserved. No part of this book may be reproduced or transmitted, in any form or by any means, electronic or mechanical, including photocopying, recording, or by any information storage and retrieval system, without permission in writing from the Publisher.

Printed in the United States of America.

Library of Congress Catalog Card Number: 92-45188.

International Standard Book Number: 0-87778-258-X.

First Printing: March 1993.

ABOUT THE AUTHORS

Roger Kaufman (Ph.D., New York University) is Professor and Director, Center for Needs Assessment and Planning at the Florida State University. He is also associated with the faculty of industrial engineering and management systems at the University of Central Florida. Before university affiliations, he was assistant to the vice president for engineering at Douglas Aircraft, and a supervisor in Human Factors at Martin-Baltimore and Boeing.

He consults worldwide in needs assessment, strategic planning, quality management and evaluation. He has authored more than 24 books and 135 articles in these areas. A past president of the National Society for Performance and Instruction, he has been awarded their highest honor: member-for-life. He is a fellow of the American Psychological Association, and a diplomate of the American Board of Professional Psychology.

Alicia M. Rojas (Ph.D., Florida State University) is currently the Instructional Quality Program Manager for the Education Group at Tandem Computers, Inc. She has experience in the academic world as well as in the public sector.

She has consulted throughout Latin America, the Caribbean, Africa, and the United States in evaluation, strategic planning, needs assessment, and instructional design. She is an active member of NSPI at the international as well as local levels.

Hanna Mayer (Ph.D., Florida State Univesity) is President of Hanna Mayer & Associates. She specializes in needs assessment, strategic planning, organizational change management, and quality improvement, and she is an ISO 9000/quality systems auditor. She also teaches graduate courses on program planning and on consulting skills, at the Ontario Institute for Studies in Education, University of Toronto.

Her experience includes work for business and industry, education, health care, and government in Canada, the United States, and Australia. She has authored several articles and frequently presents papers, seminars, and workshops at professional conferences and meetings. She is a past vice-president of NSPI and continues to be an active member of this professional society at the international and local levels.

ACKNOWLEDGMENTS

No book dealing with something as important and as complex as this one can be done alone or in isolation. We thank our many professional colleagues, clients, and students who have helped shape our thinking and work.

Special thanks to Lawrence Lipsitz of Educational Technology Publications who has contributed to our thinking and this book.

We wish to thank Technomic Publishing Company for granting permission to use graphics from Kaufman (1988) *Planning Educational Systems*, and from Kaufman and Herman (1991) *Strategic Planning in Education*. Also, our appreciation to Sage Publishing and Corwin Press for allowing us to use graphics from Kaufman (1992) *Strategic Planning Plus*, and *Mapping Educational Success*.

We also thank Jean Van Dyke for extensive word processing and Jason Strickland for work on graphics.

Roger Kaufman
Tallahassee, Florida

Alicia M. Rojas
Mountain View, California

Hanna Mayer
Toronto, Canada

Table of Contents

Chapter 1

      NEEDS ASSESSMENT: THE BASICS   1

Chapter 2

      MEGA-LEVEL NEEDS ASSESSMENT   23

Chapter 3

      MACRO-LEVEL NEEDS ASSESSMENT   51

Chapter 4

      MICRO-LEVEL NEEDS ASSESSMENT   77

Chapter 5

      QUASI NEEDS ASSESSMENT   99

Chapter 6

      NEEDS ASSESSMENT AND
      ORGANIZATIONAL EFFECTIVENESS   123

Chapter 7

      A NEEDS ASSESSMENT TOOL KIT   141

Bibliography   181

Index   185

Introduction

This book is for anyone involved in planning, management, administration, organizational change, assessment, evaluation, and renewal. It is for: people who must decide where to go and justify why; those who conduct needs assessments; those who supervise or use the information from needs assessments: administrators, managers, executives. It provides professionals with advice on the type of needs assessment they should use, why, and how. The book provides an explanation of different types of needs assessments, when each is most appropriate to use, and how to successfully conduct each type of needs assessment.

By using the correct needs assessment approach and by working with the results and recommendations derived from it, you and your organization will be able to:

- Assure that you are heading in the right direction.
- Have justifications for doing, changing, or revising your own as well as your organization's accomplishments.
- Identify the real problems and opportunities your organization faces, and select appropriate methods, means, solutions, and interventions that will deliver the results you have to have.
- Ensure that you will be accountable for the right things, and not engage in incorrect or inappropriate actions and quick-fixes (for which you are likely to be blamed).
- Have assurance that you will be doing the right things, not just doing things right...by correctly relating ends and means.

Examples, cases-in-point, and checklists are provided to allow you to:

- Identify the basics of doing a needs assessment.
- List the steps for doing one.
- Learn how to apply this process in any organization—both in the private and public sectors.

Organizational life is not linear or lock-step...needs assessment should not be rigid either. This book allows you to select the type of needs assessment (including appropriate tools and techniques) for several different varieties. Instead of leading the reader through each chapter, this book is written so that you can go directly to various options depending upon your questions and the scope you require (see Job Aid). We do, however, recommend that you start with the Mega level —"biggest-picture"—needs assessment approach, as it offers the largest, most complete scope of needs assessment (see Chapter 2).

The following is a short outline of the contents of each of the following chapters in this book.

Chapter One. The Basics

Needs assessments: what they are and what they will do for you.

The chapter explains and discusses: six questions which any organization should ask and answer; three levels of results for which needs assessments can help; the vital "secret of needs assessment"—relating ends and means; payoffs and consequence of conducting needs assessment at the Mega, Macro, and Micro levels; the definition of Quasi Needs Assessment; the steps to follow when conducting needs assessment at the different levels. References and readings are suggested.

Chapter Two. Mega-level Needs Assessment

When the primary client and beneficiary is the organization's clients and the external world, use a Mega-level Needs Assessment.

The chapter describes and explains what Mega-level Needs Assessment is; why and when it should be used; what are the steps, tools, and techniques one could use when doing it. Examples, checklists, and application tools such as forms are provided. References and readings are suggested.

Chapter Three. Macro-level Needs Assessment

When the primary client and beneficiary is the organization itself, use a Macro-level Needs Assessment.

The chapter specifies and explains what Macro-level Needs Assessment is; why and when it should be used; what are the steps, tools, and techniques one could use when doing one. Examples, checklists, and application tools such as forms are provided. References and readings are suggested.

Needs Assessment—Introduction

	IF you are	THEN read
1.	Interested in learning as much as you can about Needs Assessment?	All chapters
2.	Concerned with the usefulness to both external clients and society?	Chapter 1—The Basics, & Chapter 2—Megal-level Needs Assessment
3.	Concerned with the quality of what your organization delivers to its external clients?	Chapter 1—The Basics, & Chapter 3—Macro-level Needs Assessment
4.	Interested in the quality of what is turned out within your organization and is used by internal clients?	Chapter 1—The Basics, & Chapter 4—Micro-level Needs Assessment
5.	Interested in the efficiency of your organization's activities, operations, and resources?	Chapter 5—Quasi Needs Assessment (or Methods-Means Analysis)
6.	Concerned with training requirements?	Chapter 5—Quasi Needs Assessment
7.	Interested in learning the procedures of how to satisfy an identified need?	Chapter 5—Quasi Needs Assessment
8.	Concerned with the quality and availability of your human, capital, and material resources?	Chapter 5—Quasi Needs Assessment
9.	Interested in the relationship between Needs Assessment and planning?	Chapter 6—Organizational Effectiveness and Needs Assessment

Job Aid. Where to go in this book based on your own interest or work requirements.

Chapter Four. Micro-level Needs Assessment

When the primary client and beneficiary is the organization's internal clients, use a Micro-level Needs Assessment.

The chapter describes and explains: what Micro-level Needs Assessment is; why and when it should be used; what are the steps, tools, and techniques one could use when doing one. Needs, Opportunities, and Maintenance: A NOM Assessment. Examples, checklists, and application tools such as forms are provided. References and readings are suggested.

Chapter Five. Quasi Needs Assessment

When you are interested in finding out the most efficient tools, techniques, interventions, and resources, you may do a Quasi Needs Assessment.

The chapter is structured to describe and explain what a Quasi Needs Assessment is; why and when it should be used; what are the steps, tools, and techniques one could use when doing it. Examples, checklists, and application tools such as forms are provided. References and readings are suggested.

Chapter Six. Needs Assessment and Organizational Effectiveness

The chapter includes discussions regarding organizational efforts, results, consequences, and payoffs; strategic planning, strategic planning plus, and the role of needs assessment; roll-up versus roll-down planning; effectiveness and efficiency; utility and usefulness. References and readings are suggested.

Chapter Seven. Tool Kit

Additional guides, tools, and forms. References and readings are suggested.

A Preview of What's Coming Your Way

If assessing needs were really a simple matter, no book or set of guidelines would be necessary...you would simply list the objectives you want to accomplish and go after them. But humans are complex, and so are the organizations they set up, work in, and derive results from. Don't kid yourself. If something to do with human behavior seems too simple to be true, it probably is! While the call for keeping things simple is certainly important, let's not oversimplify things to the point where we don't get the success we must define and deliver.

Nevertheless, needs assessment is not difficult to understand and put to use. It isn't mathematical, or mysterious. Doing a needs assessment properly will allow you to define where you should be headed, justify why you are going there, and what is the best way to get there. Needs assessments entail using a systematic process for identifying problems and opportunities for improvement, and making important decisions about addressing them. Needs assessments are more than just questionnaires sent to supervisors and workers, or sitting around with some smart people and deciding what to do.

We are going to walk you through the major aspects of needs assessments so that you will be able to know what they are, and what types exist; provide questions to help you select the right approach; and identify methods and tools for getting the job done with the least amount of fuss while delivering the basic information you must have to make your organization effective and efficient.

Following are the major terms and concepts we cover in this book. Most of them won't mean much to you now, but they will become meaningful when you have finished the book. Use them as a checklist of your progress and knowledge about needs assessment. We will highlight the terms and concepts we present in each chapter.

Checklist of major terms and concepts explained in this book

>   NEEDS
>   NEEDS ASSESSMENT
>   QUASI NEEDS
>   QUASI NEEDS ASSESSMENT
>   NEEDS ASSESSMENT (AND PLANNING) PARTNERSHIPS
>
>   MEANS
>   ENDS
>
>   GOALS
>   OBJECTIVES
>   ORGANIZATIONAL ELEMENTS
>   INPUTS
>   PROCESSES
>   PRODUCTS
>   OUTPUTS
>   OUTCOMES
>   ORGANIZATIONAL ELEMENTS MODEL (OEM)

PLANNING
UTILITY
EFFECTIVENESS
EFFICIENCY

MEGA
MACRO
MICRO

ROLL-DOWN
ROLL-UP
SOCIETAL REALITIES AND OPPORTUNITIES
STRATEGIC PLANNING
STRATEGIC PLANNING PLUS
TOTAL QUALITY MANAGEMENT
TOTAL QUALITY MANAGEMENT "PLUS"

EVALUATION
REACTIVE
PROACTIVE

NEEDS ANALYSIS
FRONT-END ANALYSIS
PERFORMANCE ANALYSIS
PROBLEM ANALYSIS
GOAL ANALYSIS
"TRAINING NEEDS ASSESSMENT"
NEEDS, OPPORTUNITIES, AND MAINTENANCE
    (NOM) ANALYSIS

NEEDS ASSESSMENT: THE BASICS

Chapter 1

Key points:

- What needs assessments are and what they will do for you.

- Six questions which any organization should ask and answer.

- Three levels of results which needs assessments can target.

- The differences and relationships among ends and means—the vital "secret" of needs assessments.

- Payoffs and consequences of conducting needs assessment at the Mega, Macro, and Micro levels.

- The definition of Quasi Needs Assessment.

- The steps to follow when conducting needs assessment at the different levels.

Needs Assessment: The Basics—Chapter 1

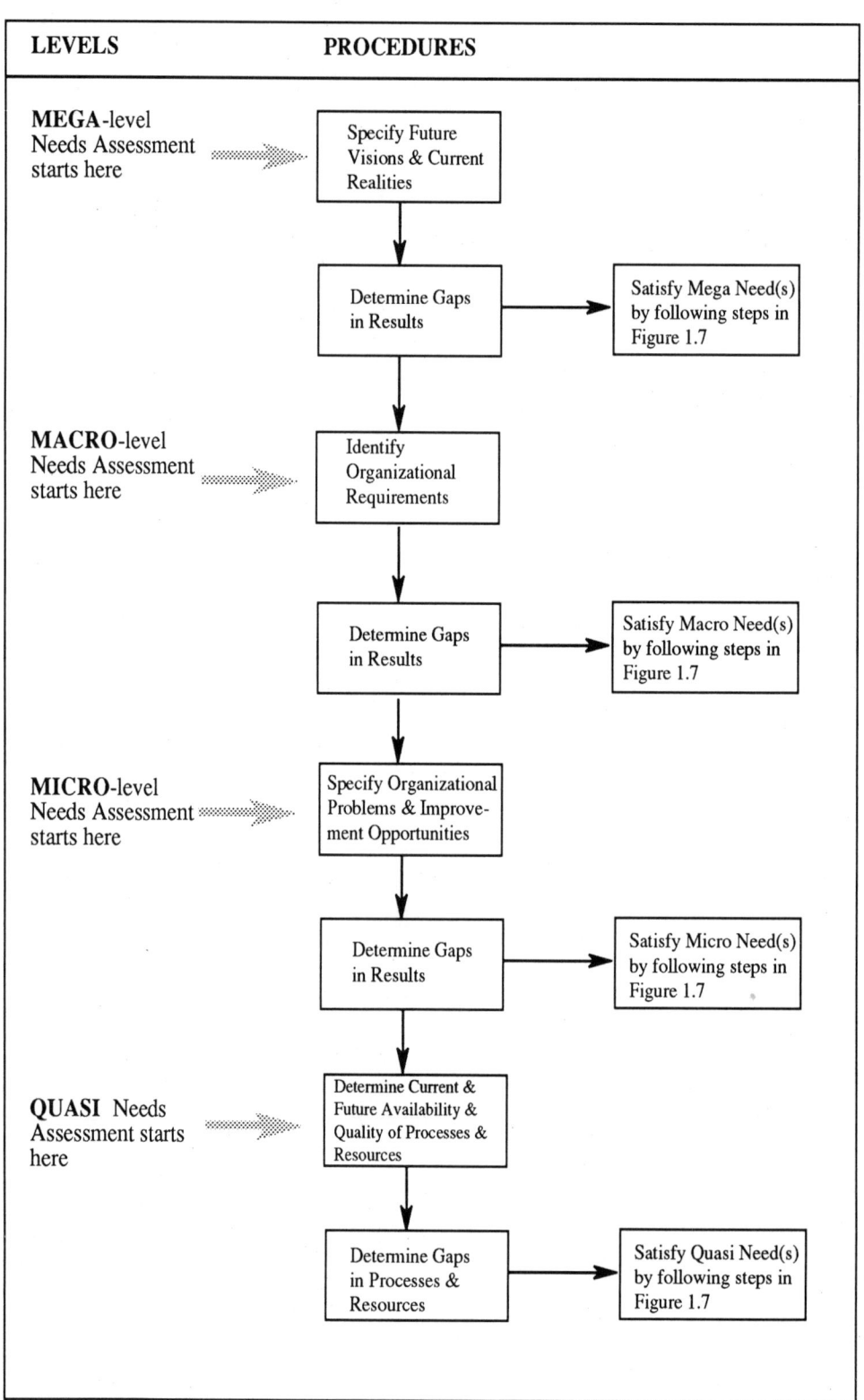

A guide to follow when conducting needs assessment at Mega, Macro, and Micro levels, and when identifying Quasi needs.

Have you ever faced any of the following questions?

- What training should we have?
- How can we improve performance?
- Are our mission objectives correct? Timely?
- How can we improve quality?
- What do we have to know in order to do a total quality management program?
- Can we improve our profits?
- Can we get more "bang for the buck"?
- Are we as effective as possible?
- Can we plan to get better results?
- Are our current goals and objectives the right ones?

If the answer is "yes" to one or more of these, then needs assessment is a useful tool for you. All of these questions center on *needs*—gaps between our current results and payoffs and those we could or should have.

This chapter will provide an overview of the needs assessment process and an explanation of related concepts, principles, and procedures.

What is Needs Assessment?

Needs Assessment is a process we use to:

- Identify gaps between current results and desired ones.
- Place the gaps in results (needs) in priority order.
- Select the most important ones to be addressed.

Once we select the most important needs to be addressed, it is important to analyze their causes (do a needs analysis). This will help in determining what it would take to resolve the selected needs.

By conducting a needs assessment, you will be able to determine where you should be going and when you have arrived there; you will know the reasons for getting to where you are headed; and you will have the basic information to analyze the needs to find their causes.

The definition of "need"

The comedian George Carlin is said to have a routine which goes something (this version is modified) like this:

A man enters a hardware store and says to the clerk "I 'need' some 1/4 inch drills." The clerk answers "You don't 'need' 1/4 inch drills, you really *want* 1/4 inch *holes!*"

This, as only humor sometimes can do, highlights the important difference between ends (the 1/4 inch holes) and means (1/4 inch drills). Of course, the clerk wants to sell drills...but points out that the ends are holes and the likely means to get those holes are drills. People who make their money on means are often not likely to point out the ends/means relationship.

As simple as this ends/means distinction is—and how utterly basic and critical it is to differentiate ends from means—most people mistakenly intermix them. In order to be useful, a needs assessment must be ends-focused, and it must provide the hard evidence required to allow one to select the most effective and efficient means-to-the-ends.

Needs assessment is a very valuable tool for identifying where you are—the current results and consequences—and where you should be—the desired results and consequences. If we are to assess needs, we have to know what the needs are.

Needs are gaps in results, consequences, or accomplishments (Figure 1.1).

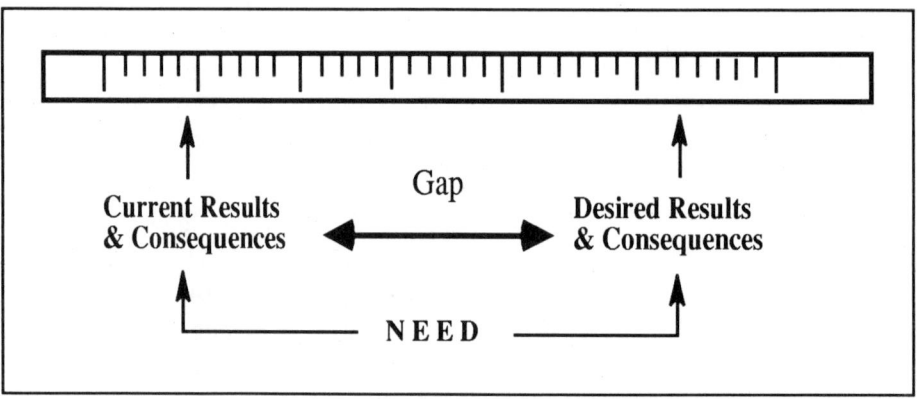

Figure 1.1. Needs are gaps in results.

Once the needs are identified, they may sensibly be placed in priority order. Based upon the prioritized needs, you then select the best ways to get from here to there. Means are the ways—i.e., solutions, methods, interventions, programs, activities—to close the gaps and thus to meet the needs (Figure 1.2).

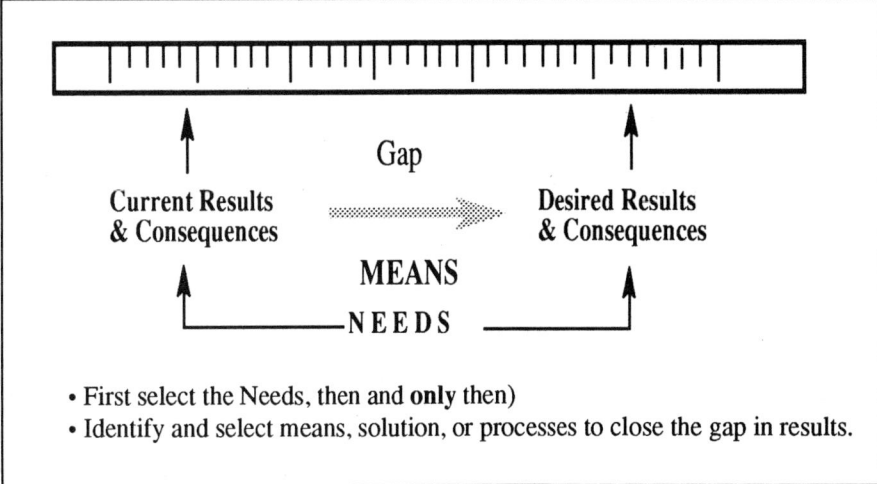

Figure 1.2. Means are the ways to meet the needs.

It is all quite sensible and practical. If there are no gaps between the results and consequences of what you now deliver, and what you should deliver, you have no needs. You simply keep on doing whatever you are doing. If there are gaps (discrepancies), it is time to find a way to close those gaps in *results.*

A needs assessment tells you:

- What results, payoffs, and consequences you now get.
- What results, payoffs, and consequences you should get.
- Why you should get the new results, payoffs, and consequences.
- The priorities for the needs: which gaps in results you should close and in what order.

Let's examine why you may decide to do needs assessments, what you can accomplish by conducting needs assessments, what makes the process of assessing needs useful and practical, and what tools and techniques you can use to answer important organizational questions.

Six questions which any organization should ask and answer

Any organization, in either the private or public sector, has several questions which it must ask and answer (Kaufman, 1992a, b; Kaufman and Herman, 1991). Often, these questions are not directly confronted, but they exist all the same. (Ignoring something really does not make it go away.) These questions can be vital to you in:

- Identifying where you are (in terms of results, payoffs, and value).
- Identifying where you should be (again, in terms of results, payoffs, and value).
- Determining if and when you have successfully made the journey from here to there.

Here are the questions. Ask them of your own organization:

Question 1 Do you care about the impact and contribution your organization makes to external clients and society?

Question 2 Do you care about the quality of what your organization delivers to external clients?

Question 3 Do you care about the quality of what your organization delivers to internal clients?

Question 4 Do you care about the efficiency of your operations and activities?

Question 5 Do you care about the quality and availability of your human, capital, and material resources?

Question 6 Do you care about the extent to which you have reached your objectives and/or about the value and worth of your methods?

Questions 1, 2, and 3 are concerned with results—impacts, consequences, accomplishments. Questions 4 and 5 focus on means, resources, and how-to-do-its. Question 6, not directly covered in this book, deals with evaluation. Every organization should formally and specifically deal with each of these questions. Based on the answers, differential gaps between current results and payoffs and desired results and payoffs will be determined.

Here is how this works:

Three levels of results

Any organization has three levels of results (Kaufman, 1992a, b):

1. **External/Societal Contribution:** The impacts, payoffs, and consequences for all external clients.
2. **Organization Outputs:** The quality of that which they can or do deliver outside of the organization.
3. **Internal Products:** The impacts, payoffs, and consequences for all internal clients.

Each of these relate to the first three questions in Table 1.1.

Question	Primary Recipients	Consequences
Question 1. Do you care about the impact and contribution your organization makes to external clients and society?	Societal and external clients	Impact on external client and societal payoffs and quality of life
Question 2. Do you care about the quality of what your organization delivers to external clients?	The organization itself	External client satisfaction
Question 3. Do you care about the quality of what your organization delivers to internal clients?	Internal clients, i.e., individuals and/or groups within the organization	Internal client satisfaction; impact on internal staff morale

Table 1.1. Questions to be asked and answered in any needs assessment and planning effort, and each one's primary recipients and consequences.

The three levels of results depend upon which is the primary client and primary beneficiary (Kaufman, 1992a). For each see Table 1.2.

Table 1.2. Levels of needs assessment based upon who is the primary client and beneficiary. (Based on Kaufman, 1992a.)

Who is the primary client and beneficiary?	Needs Assessment Level
Society, Community, External Clients	MEGA
The Organization Itself	MACRO
Individuals and/or Small Groups	MICRO

Needs Assessment in context: Levels and choices

There are three needs assessment levels, and they do relate one to the other, whether formally realized or not. Figure 1.3 shows these relationships. Also shown are the interrelationships among results at the three levels.

We recommend the Mega level be the preferred choice. Since we realize that not everyone will select it, we discuss Mega-, Macro-, and Micro-level Needs Assessments. The choice, of course, is yours to make.

There are special considerations which are unique to each organization. For example, the US Department of Energy's Oak Ridge Associated Universities emphasizes the importance of the environment (which doesn't stop at any artificial political boundary such as a state or nation) as shown in Figure 1.4.

When working with clients, the development of unique frameworks such as these can be useful in understanding the importance of the several layers, or levels, for needs assessment.

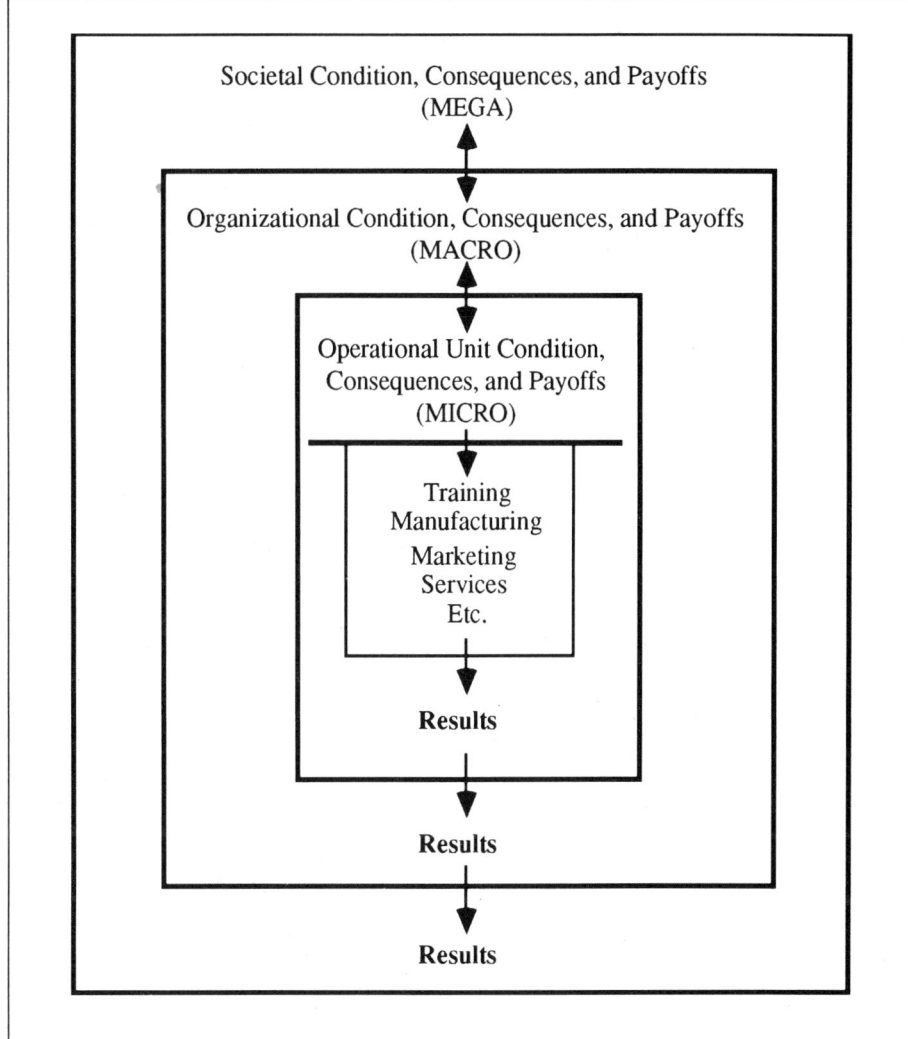

Figure 1.3. Three major frameworks for needs assessment and planning. The two-way arrows indicate interrelationships. Notice that the results from the Micro level lead to those at the Macro level, and those results in turn lead to results at the Mega level.

Needs Assessment and Quasi Needs Assessment

Needs assessment is the process for identifying gaps in results. Quasi Needs Assessment is the process for identifying methods-means, procedures, and how-to-do-its. Quasi Needs Assessment also identifies gaps in the availability and/or quality of human, capital, and other resources used by individuals and organizations.

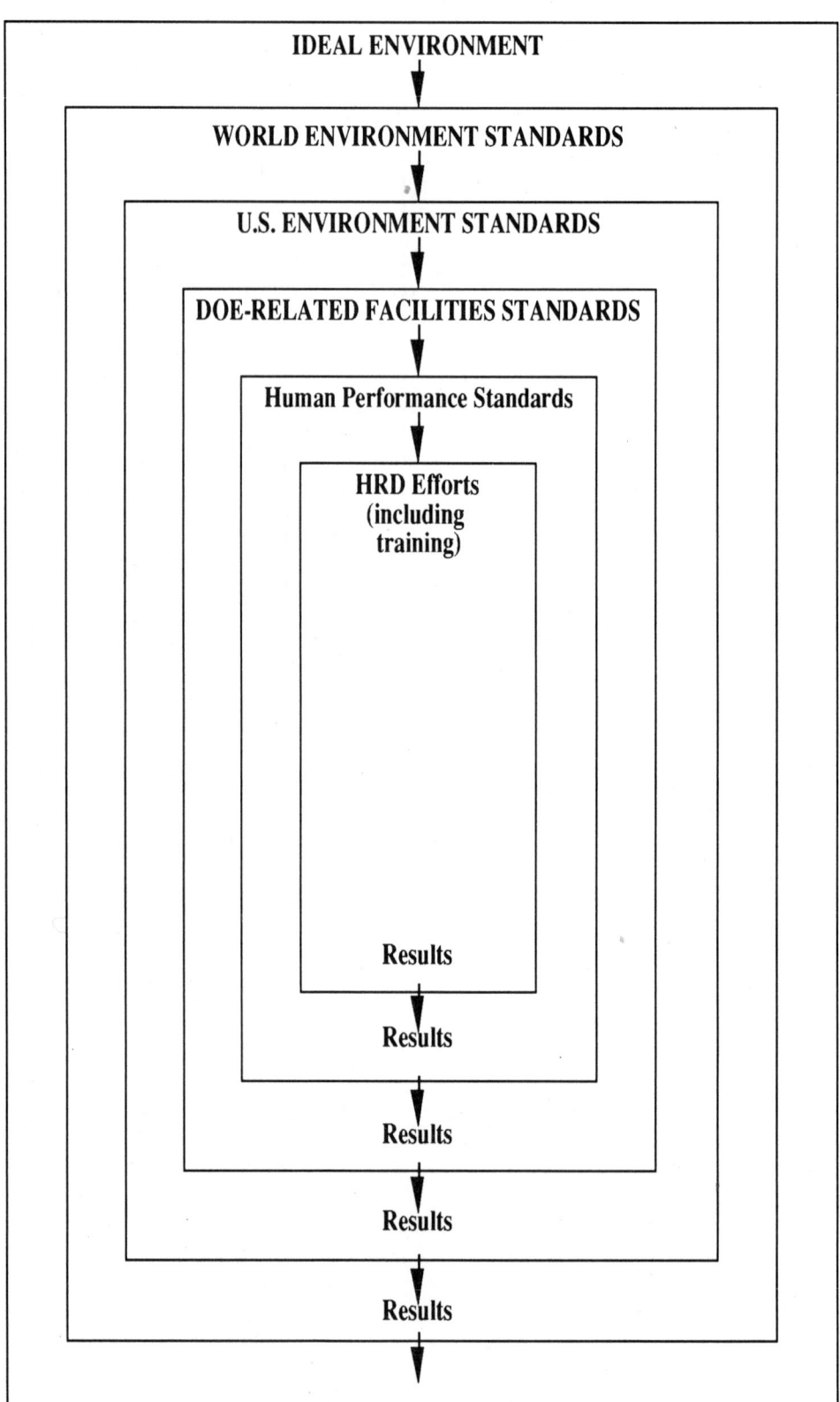

Figure 1.4. Framework consideration for needs assessment for the US Department of Energy as developed by the Oak Ridge Associated Universities for purposes of needs assessment and planning. (With permission.)

Table 1.3 summarizes the relationship among the questions, the primary recipients, and the assessment level.

Table 1.3. Quasi Needs Assessment questions.

Question	Primary Recipients & Consequences	Needs Assessment Level
Question 4. Do you care about the efficiency of your operations and activities?	The quality and efficiency of processes	Quasi Needs Assessment
Question 5. Do you care about the quality of and availability of your human, capital, and material resources?	The quality of inputs	Quasi Needs Assessment

The Organization Elements Model (OEM): Three types of results and two types of means and resources

A useful template, or pattern, when doing needs assessment is a framework which identifies three levels of results (Mega, Macro, and Micro) and two elements composed of means (Processes) and resources (Inputs) (Quasi needs). This five-part framework is called the OEM—Organizational Elements Model (Kaufman, 1988, 1992a, b).

Any organization—public or private—may be described as using these five elements. Figure 1.5 shows the five elements of the OEM: Inputs, Processes, Products, Outputs, and Outcomes along with examples of each.

The levels of needs assessment relate to the organizational elements: Outcomes are results at the MEGA level; Outputs are results at the MACRO level; Products are results at the MICRO level. See the relationships in Table 1.4.

Typical **Outcomes** for clients, and consequences for Question 1 (Table 1.1) include the safety, self-sufficiency, and quality of life for mill workers; the continuing income and well-being of graduates; the profits earned and

ORGANIZATIONAL ELEMENT	INPUTS (Resources, means)	PROCESSES (Interventions, methods)	PRODUCTS (En-route results, the performance, "building blocks")	OUTPUTS (The aggregated products of the system which are delivered or deliverable to society)	OUTCOMES (The effects of outputs in and for society and the client)
EXAMPLES	Existing human resources; existing needs; goals; objectives; policies; regulations; money; values; laws; societal and client characteristics; current quality of life.	Procedures; total quality management program; teaching; learning; human resources development; training; selling; managing; manufacturing; marketing.	Course completed; competency test passed; inspection approved; fender completed; surgery completed; loans approved.	Delivered automobiles; sold computer systems; program completers; job completed; bill mailed to client; patients discharged; graduates; houses ready for escrow.	Safety of outputs continued; profit; dividend declared; continued funding; self-sufficient; self-reliant; productive individual; socially competent and effective; contributing to self and other; no crime; financial independence.
NEEDS ASSESSMENT LEVEL	QUASI	QUASI	MICRO	MACRO	MEGA
PRIMARY CLIENT AND BENEFICIARY			Individuals and groups within the organization	The organization itself	Societal and external clients

Figure 1.5. Relationships and examples of the Organizational Element Model (OEM).

Level/Scope of Planning & Needs Assessment	Primary Client and Beneficiary	Organizational Elements
MEGA	Society/Community	Outcomes
MACRO	The organization itself	Outputs
MICRO	Individuals and small groups	Products

Table 1.4. Relating level/scope of planning and needs assessment, primary clients and beneficiaries, and the results elements of the OEM.

reputation of a Fortune 500 company, and no violations of environmental laws.

Typical **Outputs** for Question 2 (Table 1) include automobiles delivered to customers; patients discharged from a hospital or mental care institution; learners graduated from a community college.

Typical **Products** for Question 3 (Table 1.1) include fenders assembled which meet quality standards; a successful gall bladder operation; a geometry course that was completed.

How does the OEM relate to Needs Assessment?

The OEM can be related to needs and needs assessment by viewing it as a two-level framework (Kaufman, 1988, 1992a). Figure 1.6 shows the OEM and its relation to "What Is" and "What Should Be." Because there are three types of needs (Outcomes, Outputs, Products) there are three types of needs assessments. Because there are two types of quasi needs (Processes, Inputs) there are two types of Quasi Needs Assessments.

Figure 1.6. The Organizational Elements Model (OEM) as a two-tiered framework for identifying "What Is" and "What Should Be." (Based on Kaufman, 1992a.)

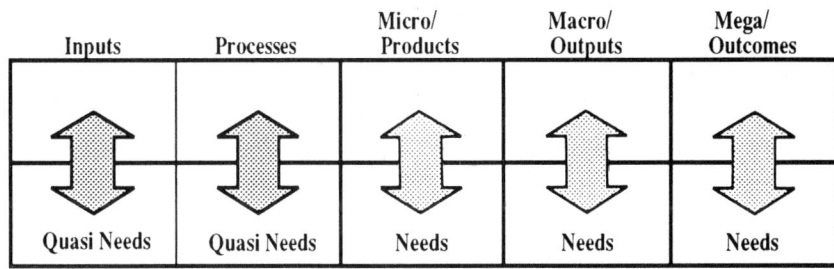

In summary, for each Organizational Element there is a needs assessment level as specified in Table 1.5.

Table 1.5. Relationships among Organizational Elements and Needs Assessment Levels.

Organizational Element	Needs Assessment Level
Outcome	Mega Needs Assessment
Output	Macro Needs Assessment
Product	Micro Needs Assessment
Process	Quasi Needs Assessment
Input	Quasi Needs Assessment

How to do Needs Assessment

We recommend a sequence of generic steps to follow, as shown in Figure 1.7.

Note, however, that the specific steps for conducting needs assessments are somewhat varied, depending on the level of needs assessment (or Quasi Needs Assessment) you decide to apply and use. The steps for conducting each of the three needs assessment levels (Mega, Macro, and Micro) and for conducting a quasi needs assessment are listed below. They are discussed in detail in the following chapters (2, 3, 4, and 5).

Mega-level Needs Assessment steps

The seven major steps for conducting a **Mega-level Needs Assessment** (explained in detail in Chapter 2) include:

1. Determine your organization's **ideal vision**, including indicators of its impact on the survival and quality of life of its external clients and society.
2. Determine your organization's **current status** with regard to its impact on clients' and society's survival and quality of life.
3. Place Mega-level gaps (i.e., Needs) between your ideal vision and the current status, in a priority order, based on the cost to ignore vs. the cost to successfully address each identified need.
4. Write a *realistic* mission objective which includes a specific sub-objective for each gap you decided to address (e.g., what you will have accomplished five or more years from now).
5. Break down your mission objective to functional building-block objectives.
6. Present your Mega-level needs to your clients for concurrence.
7. Identify and list alternative methods and means for addressing your Mega-level need(s) and identify the advantages and disadvantages of each.

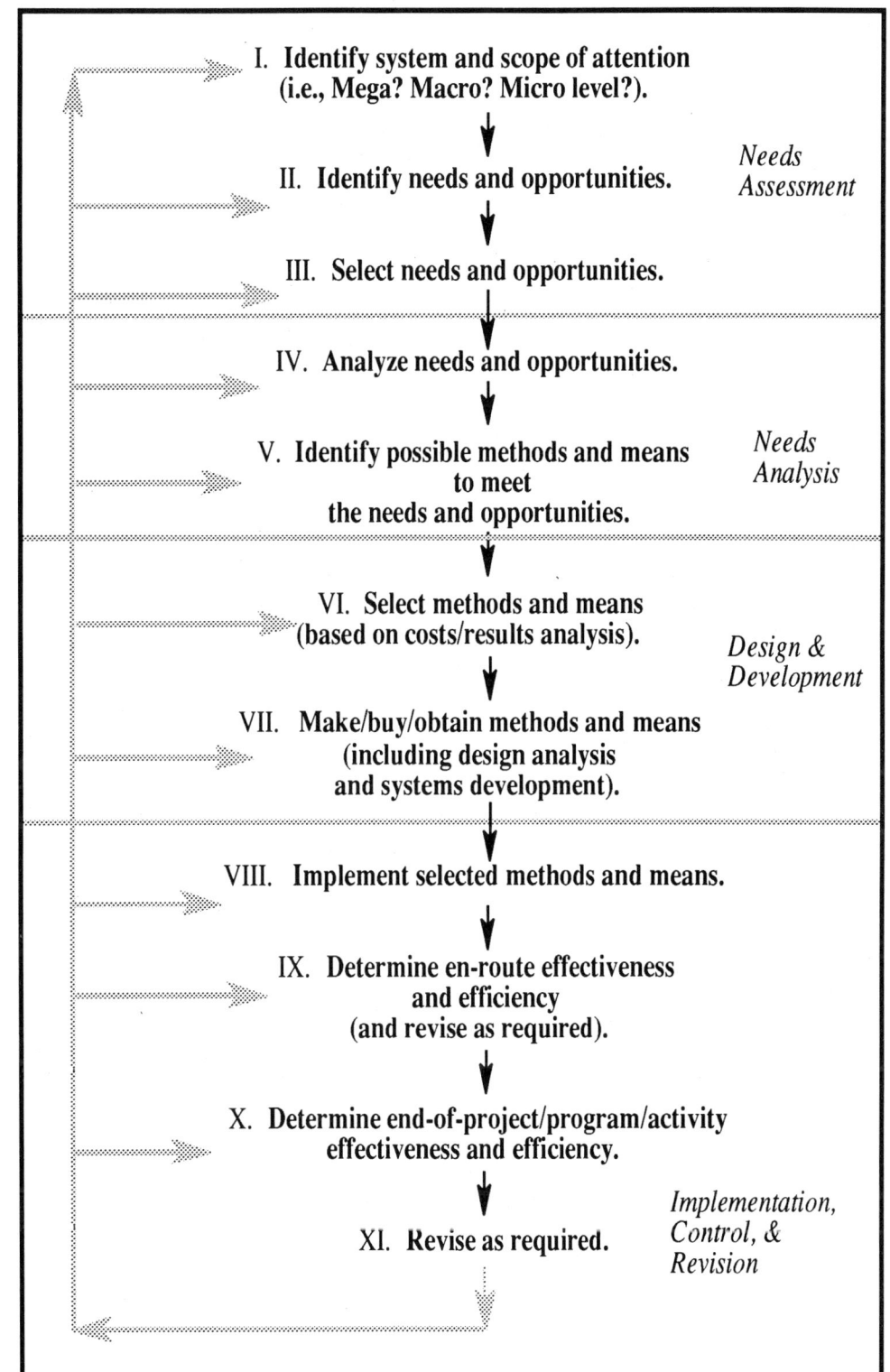

Figure 1.7. Sequence of generic needs assessment steps and their relationship to analysis, design and development, implementation and control, evaluation and revision. This sequence of steps may be applied to the different levels of needs assessment.

Macro-level Needs Assessment steps

The seven major steps for conducting a **Macro-level Needs Assessment** (explained in detail in Chapter 3) include:

1. Determine the desired quality of what your organization delivers to external clients.
2. Determine the current quality of what your organization delivers to external clients.
3. List the identified, agreed upon need(s).
4. Align the needs identified at the Macro level with the Vision and Mission of your organization.
5. Place Macro-level needs in a priority order, based on the cost to ignore versus the cost to address each identified need.
6. Present your Macro-level needs to your clients for concurrence.
7. Identify and list alternative methods and means for addressing your Macro-level need(s) and identify the advantages and disadvantages of each.

Micro-level Needs Assessment steps

The seven major steps for conducting a **Micro-level Needs Assessment** (explained in detail in Chapter 4) include:

1. Determine individuals' and/or groups' required performance in terms of measurable accomplishments.
2. Determine individuals' and/or groups' current performance status vis-a-vis the required standards established in step 1.
3. List the identified, agreed upon Micro-level need(s).
4. Align the needs identified at the Micro level with the Vision and Mission of your organization.
5. Place Micro-level needs in priority order, based on the cost to ignore versus the cost to address each identified need.
6. Present your Micro-level needs to your clients for concurrence.
7. Identify and list alternative methods and means for addressing your Micro-level need(s), and identify the advantages and disadvantages of each.

Quasi Needs Assessment steps

The nine major steps for conducting a **Quasi Needs Assessment** (explained in detail in Chapter 5) include:

1. Specify the desired availability and/or quality of the organizational resources and methods.
2. Determine the current quality and/or availability of the organizational efforts.
3. Determine Quasi needs—the gaps between the desired and the current organizational efforts.
4. Align the Quasi needs identified with the Needs at Mega, Macro, and Micro levels.
5. Place Quasi need(s) in order of importance, based on the cost to ignore versus the cost to address each identified quasi need.
6. (or Step 1 if you have already identified needs at Mega, Macro, and/or Micro levels). Identify alternative methods and means for addressing the identified Quasi need(s) and/or need(s).
7. (or Step 2 if you have already identified needs at the Mega, Macro, and/or Micro levels). Identify advantages and disadvantages of each possible method and means available to get the job done.
8. (or Step 3 if you have already identified needs at the Mega, Macro, and/or Micro levels). Identify constraints and eliminate them if possible.
9. Present alternative methods and means for addressing all agreed upon needs and Quasi needs to your clients, and obtain concurrence on the methods and means to be selected for action.

Needs Assessment (and planning) partnerships

If important and representative people are not part of any needs assessment and planning effort — if they don't help define where they and the organization are headed, why they are going there, and how to tell when they have arrived — they will not likely allow change to come about. They can block change in many subtle and overt ways. A sure way to get people out of their comfort zones, regardless of how sensible the suggested changes, is to alienate them from the planning partnership. Peter Drucker (1973) refers to the handing off of any plans, programs, or activities to those who will be affected by them as transfer of ownership.

Everyone doesn't have to be physically part of the needs assessment and planning partnership, but they should all feel that their interests, perspectives, and expertise have been represented in the process. Usually, a stratified random sample of the internal and external clients as well as other organizational employees—recipients and implementers—should be part of any needs assessment process (as well as strategic planning and total quality management activities).

As you go through the next chapters on needs assessments at the Mega, Macro, Micro, and Quasi levels, realize that what we recommend is to be accomplished by a needs assessment planning team. The details, if you want them, of setting up a needs assessment and planning team are provided in Chapter 7.

Chapter Summary

Need is defined as gaps in results, consequences, or accomplishments.

Needs assessments:

- Identify gaps between current results and desired ones (Needs).
- Place the needs in priority order.
- Select the ones to be addressed.

Needs assessment reveals where you should be going and how to know when you have arrived. It also provides the reasons for getting to where you are headed. Needs assessments identify the gaps between your current accomplishments and those that you should deliver. Planners and organizational developers/improvers use needs assessment information to identify where they should be headed, why get there, and what building-block results have to be delivered to get from here to there.

Any organization has three levels of results:

1. **External/Societal Contribution (Outcomes):** The impacts, payoffs, and consequences for all external clients. These are Mega-level concerns.
2. **Organization Outputs:** The quality of that which they can or

do deliver outside of the organization. These are Macro-level concerns.

3. **Internal Products:** The impacts, payoffs, and consequences for all internal clients. These are Micro-level concerns.

Each of the levels relates to a series of questions that your own organization should be interested in addressing:

Question 1   Do you care about the impact and contribution your organization makes to external clients and society?

Question 2   Do you care about the quality of what your organization delivers to external clients?

Question 3   Do you care about the quality of what your organization delivers to internal clients?

The following important questions are not focused on results but on means, resources, and how-to-do-its:

Question 4   Do you care about the efficiency of your operations and activities?

Question 5   Do you care about the quality and availability of your human, capital, and material resources?

Based on these questions, there is a scope of needs and Quasi Needs Assessments for each Organizational Element. This is summarized in Table 1.6.

Level	What Is	What Should Be	
MEGA	Outcomes	Outcomes	Needs Assessments
MACRO	Outputs	Outputs	
MICRO	Products	Products	
Interventions	Processes	Processes	Quasi Needs Assessments
Resources	Inputs	Inputs	

Table 1.6. Comparing Needs Assessments and Quasi Needs Assessments.

References and Suggested Readings

Drucker, P. F. (1973) *Management: Tasks, responsibilities, practices.* New York: Harper & Row.

Gilbert, T. F. (1978) *Human competence: Engineering worthy performance.* New York: McGraw-Hill.

Gilbert, T. F. & Gilbert, M. B. (1989, Jan.) Performance engineering: Making human productivity a science. *Performance and Instruction.*

Harless, J. H. (1975) *An ounce of analysis is worth a pound of cure.* Newnan, GA: Harless Performance Guild.

Kanter, R. M. (1989) *When giants learn to dance: Mastering the challenges of strategy, management, and careers in the 1990s.* New York: Simon & Schuster.

Kaufman, R. (1987, Oct.) A needs assessment primer. *Training & Development Journal.*

Kaufman, R. (1988, Sept.) Preparing useful performance indicators. *Training & Development Journal.*

Kaufman, R. (1988) *Planning educational systems: A results-based approach.* Lancaster, PA: Technomic Publishing.

Kaufman, R. (1992a) *Strategic planning plus: An organizational guide.* Newbury Park, CA: Sage Publishing.

Kaufman, R. (1992b) *Mapping educational success.* Newbury Park, CA: Corwin Press, Division of Sage Publishing.

Kaufman, R. & Herman, J. (1991) *Strategic planning in education: Rethinking, restructuring, revitalizing.* Lancaster, PA: Technomic Publishing.

Kaufman, R. & Rojas, A. (1985) *Needs assessment.* Tallahassee, FL: Florida State Department of Health and Rehabilitative Services and the Center for Needs Assessment and Planning.

Kaufman, R. & Thiagarajan, S. (1987) Identifying and specifying requirements for instruction. In R. M. Gagné (Ed.), *Instructional technology: Foundations.* Hillsdale, NJ: Lawrence Erlbaum Associates.

Kaufman, R. & Valentine, G. (1989, Nov.) Relating needs assessment and needs analysis. *Performance & Instruction.*

Mager, R. F. (1975) *Preparing instructional objectives* (2nd Ed.). Belmont, CA: David S. Lake Publishers.

Mager, R. F. & Pipe, P. (1984) *Analyzing performance problems* (2nd Ed.). Belmont, CA: Pitman.

Peters, T. (1987) *Thriving on chaos: Handbook for a management revolution.* New York: Alfred A. Knopf.

Rossett, A. (1987) *Training needs assessment.* Englewood Cliffs, NJ: Educational Technology Publications.

Rummler, G. A. & Brache, A. P. (1990) *Improving performance: How to manage the white space on the organization chart.* San Francisco, CA: Jossey-Bass.

MEGA-LEVEL NEEDS ASSESSMENT

Chapter 2

Key points:

- What is Mega-level Needs Assessment?
- When and why do a Mega-level Needs Assessment.
- Payoffs and consequences of conducting a Mega-level Needs Assessment.
- The tools, techniques, and steps to use to conduct a Mega-level Needs Assessment.

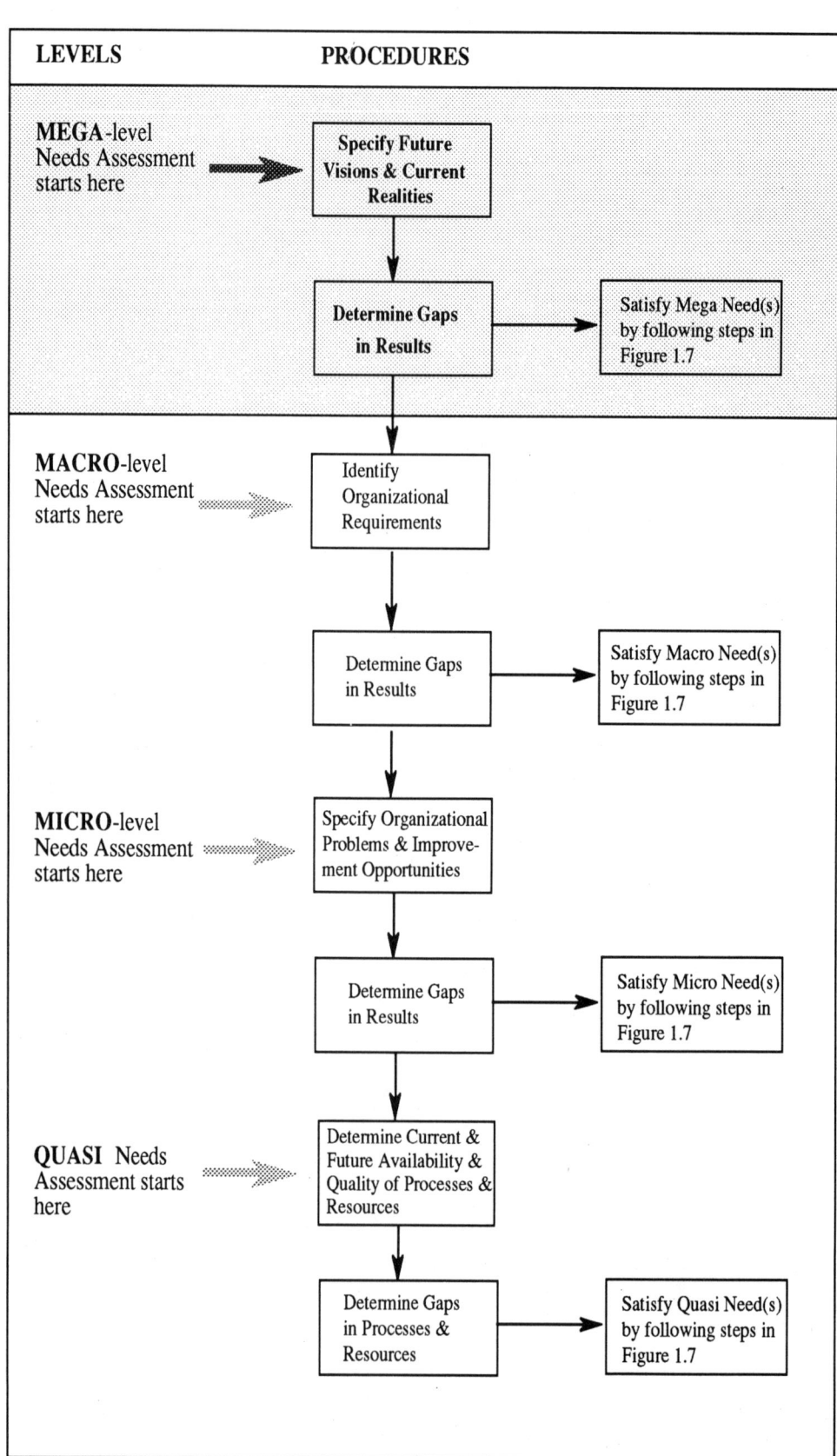

The guide to follow when conducting needs assessment at Mega, Macro, and Micro levels, and when identifying Quasi Needs. The shaded area focuses on information in this chapter.

Consider the following likely scenario:

You have just received a phone call from the Director of Human Resources of the Fort Security Company. The company is responsible for public safety at several major airports, as well as at some shopping centers and malls. Fort Security employs several hundred security guards. The company also employs some expert troubleshooters whose specialty is to successfully identify and resolve security breach situations that may endanger the safety of the public. The Director of Human Resources called you to discuss your ideas for identifying and implementing some strategies and tactics for improving the company's performance, especially the impact of Fort Security's performance on public safety (and thus also the firm's profitability).

What would you do?

The above scenario is typical. Furthermore, security companies are not the only ones concerned about the consequences of their performance on the public they ultimately serve. More and more companies are concerned about their impact on the health, safety, and quality of life in our society. More and more organizations are demanding that performance improvement strategies and tactics address societal impact concerns.

By using the correct needs assessment approach, you will be able to help organizations achieve useful results that do indeed focus on positive payoffs for society/the community.

To respond correctly and successfully to the Fort Security scenario, your approach should be to conduct a **Mega-level Needs Assessment.**

In this chapter, you will learn why this is the correct approach, when is it appropriate to do a Mega-level Needs Assessment, and what steps and procedures to take in order to do it successfully.

What is Mega-level Needs Assessment?

Mega-level Needs Assessment is a process for identifying and resolving gaps between the actual and the desired accomplishments of an organization as measured by the *usefulness* of these accomplishments to the organization's external clients and society (Drucker, 1992; Kaufman, 1992a).

For example: *Mega-level Needs Assessments may measure the extent to which an organization's accomplishments impact on:*

- Public health.
- Safety.
- The environment.
- Quality of life.
- Survival.

In the case of the Fort Security Company, the organization measures its accomplishments in terms of its impact on (improving) public safety. Fort Security is correctly addressing its possible needs at the **Mega level**.

The process of needs assessment at the Mega level is illustrated in Figure 2.1.

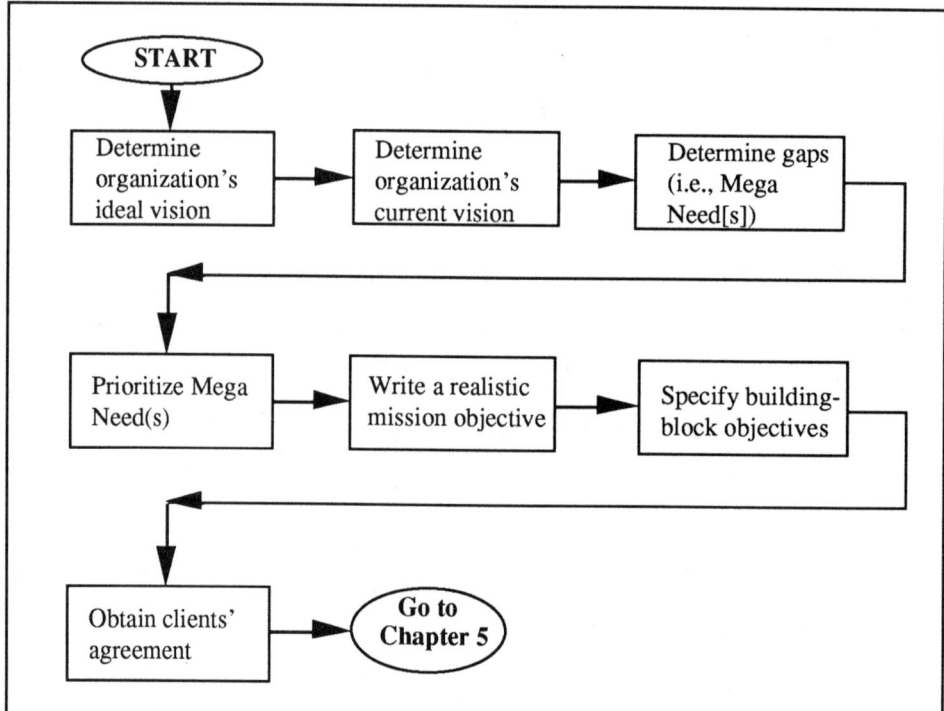

Figure 2.1. Mega-level Needs Assessment functions.

MEGA-LEVEL NEEDS ASSESSMENT—CHAPTER 2

When and why should Mega-level Needs Assessment be done?

Whenever the primary client and beneficiary of what an organization does, delivers, and serves is society itself, a Mega-level assessment is appropriate.

Whether formally recognized or not, *all* organizations impact society in some way. Organizations that do not recognize this are risking their long-term success and are probably jeopardizing their own survival.

For example: *In our scenario, Fort Security is interested in its impact on improving public safety.*

Organizations, both public and private, should ultimately think of their effect on our survival and quality of life as a society. When they do not, eventually the public reminds organizations of what considerations affect our decisions to buy (or not to buy) any available products and services.

For example: *Most breweries and distilleries have been experiencing declining sales of alcoholic drinks. The decline has been attributed to a growing concern of the public with health and safety (e.g., the risks of drinking and driving, the effects of drinking on one's health, family and friends, the caloric value of alcohol vs. its nutritional contributions). An increasing number of breweries in the U.S., Australia, and Canada are recognizing that clients' concerns with health and safety must be addressed. Some breweries have already started marketing a new non-alcoholic brand of beer. These companies took a Mega-level Needs Assessment approach. They decided that delivering a product line that is both useful and appealing to their clients is essential for their breweries' continued survival and prosperity.*

How to do a Mega-level Needs Assessment

The scope of needs assessment at the Mega level requires that special attention be given to the usefulness of the identified needs, in terms of contribution to the survival and quality of life of an organization's external clients and society.

Therefore, each of the steps for conducting a Mega-level Needs Assessment must specifically address the societal impact of what an organization does and delivers.

The following are the specific steps and procedures (best done by a needs assessment partnership group—Chapter 7) for doing a Mega-level Needs Assessment.

Step 1. Determine your organization's *ideal vision*, including indicators of its impact on the survival and quality of life of its external clients and society.

What is a vision?

A vision states the conditions you would like to achieve in the future.

An *ideal vision* states the "perfect" future—the world we want for tomorrow's child (whether or not your organization will be able to contribute to the accomplishment of the ideal vision, and whether or not the ideal vision will soon (or even ever) be reached).

With a Mega-level focus, ideal vision elements might include:

- No murders.
- No one living in poverty (or below the poverty level).
- No war.
- No deaths from AIDS.

Mega-level ideal visions tend to have much in common. After all, they all describe the same kind of world, a friendly and helpful world.

For example: *The following "draft" vision was derived by a group of community partners in Tallahassee, Florida, called "The 21st Century Council." This vision forms the basis for needs assessment and planning for the community.*

A VISION FOR TALLAHASSEE

The Tallahassee 21st Century Council is forging a partnership with all citizens of Tallahassee. Together we want to create the kind of city in which we desire our children and grandchildren to live. Tallahassee is already a good place to live...we want to make it better. Each year. We all know that we have problems. We also have opportunities. Before dealing with our current troubles, we have to first define an "ideal" Tallahassee so that we can agree on where we are as well as where we are to go.

Ours is frankly an ideal vision, one which might now seem to be beyond our practical reach. But our reach should exceed our grasp. The vision provides a shared guiding star, a distant destination towards which we want to move, day by day, year by year. By setting this "North Star" to guide us, we can develop the objectives for getting from our current status, step by step, to a much better Tallahassee when we reach the year 2000. And then, based upon our vision and progress, move beyond those accomplishments toward the ideal.

As a community of equals who value the dignity and worth of all people, we seek to cooperatively create a Tallahassee environment where:

- *All people have the opportunities, skills, and motivation enabling them to support themselves and their families.*
- *Each citizen will contribute to all other members to assure individual and community economic and social well-being and positive quality of life.*
- *All will live and work in a safe, healthful, clean, crime-free environment.*
- *All will be in good physical and mental health, free from dependence upon alcohol and drugs; their health and well-being will be such that no one will be involuntarily institutionalized by any government agency.*
- *People will neither practice nor experience discrimination based upon color, race, creed, gender, age, religion, disability, or national origin.*
- *Our community will be at the top of all US cities independently rated on quality of life.*

Will visions be different in the public vs. the private sector?

No. Visions at the Mega level will be similar regardless of whether they are done for public or private sector organizations.

For example: *The following is a vision for the hypothetical STARBUCK MOTOR COMPANY, a private sector organization.*

STARBUCK MOTOR COMPANY

The STARBUCK MOTOR COMPANY will be partners in the creation of a world which is free from murders and unintentional deaths, a poor quality of life, and which will allow current and future citizens to be self-sufficient, self-reliant, and mutually supportive. While we cannot cause it all, nor be responsible for it all, we will be "good neighbors" in assuring that the world will be a better place for all of us.

Specifically, the following vision will be achieved:

- *The air which citizens (and customers) breath will be within current air quality standards.**
- *There will be no losses of life due to design features or weaknesses from our outputs as indicated by no successful law suits based upon design defects.**
- *No one will be on welfare for more than three months.*
- *Our communities will be free of crime.*
- *There will be no deaths or illness which cause loss of work related to water quality,* sewage,* contagious disease, spouse abuse, illegal drugs, or malnutrition.*
- *There will be no discrimination in work, income, or housing (based upon court decisions) on the basis of color, race, creed, gender, life-style preference, age, religion, or national origin.*

* *Visions which are directly related to STARBUCK MOTOR COMPANY*

Why is an ideal vision important?

An ideal vision specifies the kind of world you would like your future generations to live in—without being biased by roadblocks, excuses, and conventional wisdom.

Without an "ideal," you might limit yourself to the easily achievable, though not necessarily desirable, future. With an "ideal," you will stretch towards a continuously improving future. An ideal vision is therefore not academic. It is very practical (Senge, 1990).

Does your organization have to be responsible for achieving the entire ideal vision? No. Any organization may make a contribution to the ideal vision, but it cannot reasonably deliver it all. It can, however, define what it will deliver and contribute to, as shown in Figure 2.2. Each organization can and should base its mission and purpose on an ideal vision. Based on the gaps between the ideal vision and current organizational results, needs may be identified.

When strategic planning includes the Mega level—future societal payoffs and contributions of the achievement of an ideal vision—it is termed "strategic planning plus." (Kaufman, 1992a, b.)

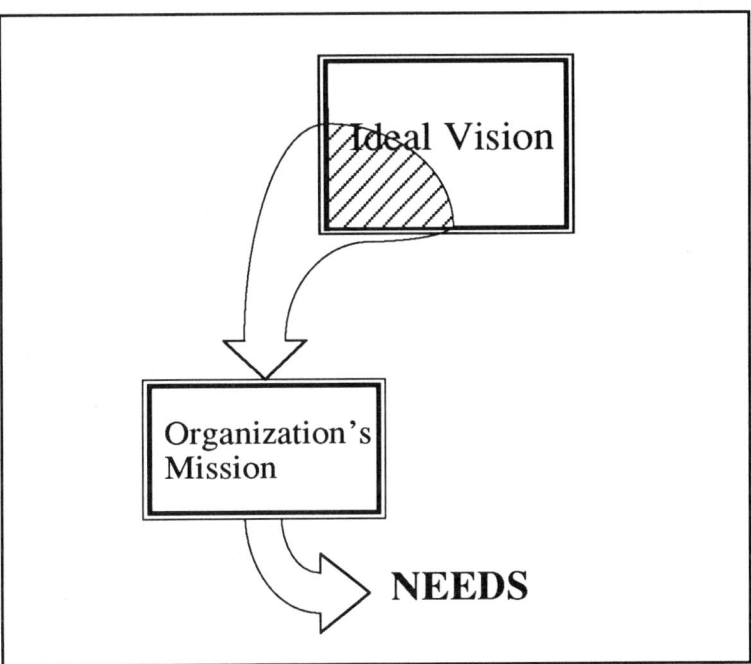

Figure 2.2. An organization's mission selects the part of the ideal vision it will deliver. (Based in part on Kaufman, 1992a, b. With permission.)

How to create an ideal vision?

To create an ideal vision, it is useful to ask planning partners to "describe the world in which you want tomorrow's children to live."

For example: *To determine the vision for the Fort Security Company (see scenario at the beginning of this chapter), you should convene a meeting with representatives of all groups potentially affected by Fort Security's operations and accomplishments:*

- *The top executives of the Fort Security Company.*
- *A representative group of current clients of the company.*
- *A group of representatives from the community (the public).*

These people will become the planning partners for Fort Security's needs assessment and planning process. Their first task will be to determine the ideal vision. This vision will be determined through discussion of group members until a consensus is reached on a vision statement that truly reflects all planning partners' views of their ideal future world.

Table 2.1 presents the likely result of the Fort Security Company planning partners first meeting, namely Fort Security's ideal vision.[1]

Fort Security	
Ideal Vision	**Results Criteria***
There will be no loss of life due to terrorist attacks.	0 deaths due to terrorists
Our community will be free of crime.	0 crime
No one will be discriminated against on the basis of color, race, gender, age, religion or national origin.	0 discrimination
Everyone in our society will be self-sufficient (i.e., not on welfare).	100% self sufficiency

Table 2.1. Fort Security's Ideal Vision. Note that they will not be responsible for delivering it all.

*Each criterion should include measurable indicators, such as "0 crime as certified by the chief legal officers of each city."

Guidelines for creating an ideal vision for your own organization:

- Set up a Needs Assessment Partnership (see Chapter 7).
- Convene a meeting of the appropriate planning partners for your organization
- Include executives, associates, clients, and community representatives.
- Meet in a quiet location, preferably in a retreat, away from phones and other distractions.
- Help everyone to state their future vision in terms of ends, not means.
- Use Form 2.1 (provided at the end of this chapter) to discuss and arrive at your ideal vision and the criteria by which you will measure the accomplishment of this vision.

Step 2. Determine your organization's current status with regard to its impact on clients' and society's survival and quality of life.

The *current status* of the same variables you included in your ideal vision statement should include a description of both the type and extent of your Mega-level accomplishments.

For example: *For each ideal vision statement, describe the current status of the same variable, as shown in Table 2.2.*

IDEAL VISION	CURRENT STATUS
- no murders	- 35 murders in our city this year
- no one living in poverty (or below the poverty level)	- 18% of our residents live at or below poverty level
- no war	- we are facing threats and possible involvement in a war from at least 3 other countries
- no deaths from AIDS	- 72 deaths from AIDS in our city this year

Table 2.2. Deriving current status of variables included in an ideal vision.

Why specify the current status of variables included in the vision statement?

To determine where we are now, so that:

- Any gaps between the vision and our present level of accomplishments vis-a-vis that vision can be determined.

- The current accomplishments that meet the desired societal vision are maintained and will continue to be maintained without any changes.

How to determine current status

Determine the current status by collecting data (facts and figures, perceptions and opinions—*hard* and *soft* data) about each variable on your ideal vision list.

The *hard data (independently verifiable facts and figures)* are provided by performance indicators. Some of these indicators may include:

- Profit (ideally over time).
- Social acceptance (e.g., sales of public stock).
- Accidents.
- Convictions.
- Accepted deliveries of goods and services with no returns or complaints.
- Employment levels.
- Deaths.

Human partners (see Chapter 7) provide the *soft data (personal perceptions)* such as:

- Values.
- Beliefs.
- Opinions.
- Visions.
- Perceived needs.

Some sources of Mega-level data may include:

- The Census Bureau.
- Future organizations.

- Research institutes and statistics centers of major universities and of governments.
- Human services agencies.
- Published studies.

For example: *To determine the current status of the ideal vision variables of the Fort Security Company (see Table 2.1), data should be collected about each variable. Table 2.3 presents the likely result of the Fort Security Company planning partners' data collection effort, presented in their second meeting.*

Table 2.3. Fort Security partners' data collection effort.

> *The current status of the ideal vision variables of the Fort Security Company:*
>
> - *There were 13 deaths due to terrorist attacks this year.*
> - *There were 57 reported crime incidents in our community this year.*
> - *23 incidents of discrimination were reported this year because of color, gender, age, religion, or national origin.*
> - *8% of our society are currently on welfare or otherwise not self-sufficient.*[1]

Guidelines for determining the current status of your vision variables:

- Determine the appropriate data sources for each item on your vision list.
- Obtain the necessary hard and soft data on each item (results only).
- Present current status data to your group of planning partners (executives, clients, and community representatives). You may complete the form provided at the end of this chapter (Form 2.2). Use the completed form as a basis for the planning partners' group discussion.

The purpose of your discussion is to arrive at a group consensus on where you are versus where you should be in terms of the ideal vision.

Note: In this second meeting with your planning partners, you should also reach consensus about the gaps which must be addressed by your organization (see Step 3 below).

Step 3. Place Mega-level gaps (i.e., Needs) between the ideal vision and the current status, in a priority order, based on the cost to ignore vs. the cost to successfully address each identified need.

Any discrepancy between your ideal vision of the world and current accomplishments vis-a-vis that vision is a Mega-level gap (or Need). Such a gap should document discrepancies in results affecting societal issues and concerns. (See Figure 2.3.)

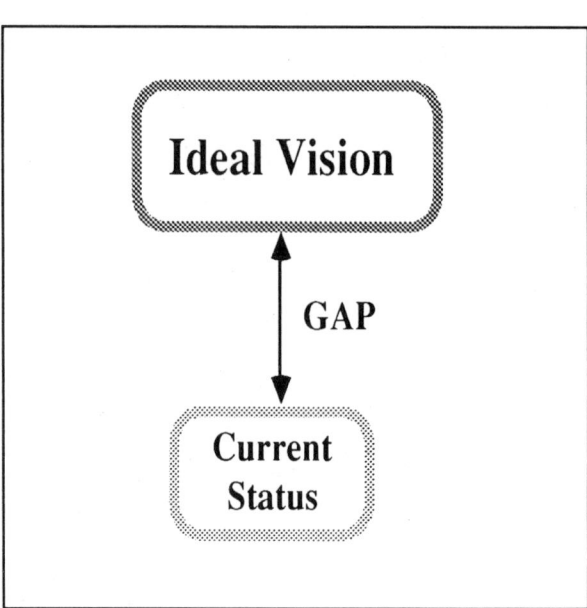

Figure 2.3. Discrepancy between ideal vision and current status.

For example: Fort Security's Mega-level needs might include:

- *Deaths* due to terrorists should be prevented by next year (there were 13 deaths this year).
- *Crime* in our community (currently 57 reported incidents) should be eliminated within the next five years.
- *Incidents of discrimination* (23 reported this year) because of color, gender, age, religion, or national origin should be eliminated within the next five years.

- *The 8% of our society who are on welfare or otherwise **not self-sufficient** will all be able to care for themselves (i.e., become self-sufficient) within the next ten years.*[1]

Why prioritize Mega-level needs?

Some needs are more critical than others. The most critical needs should be addressed more urgently than others because their consequences will be more severe.

For example: *If a gap may cause loss of life or an immediate threat to life, due to such an occurrence as terrorist bombing, it would be more important to resolve it before focusing on resolving a gap in, say, an individual's economic self-sufficiency.*

How to prioritize Mega-level needs

Prioritizing Mega-level needs requires a judgment call about the relative importance of each need. To do that, we recommend that you follow the guidelines provided below.

Guidelines for prioritizing Mega-level needs:

- Determine the criticality of each need in terms of the relative advantage (positive consequence) of addressing it, or as compared to the potential cost (negative consequence) for not addressing it. Use the following criticality benchmarks:

    Very critical: *Definitely would* contribute to improvement in public health, reduced crime, quality of life, safety at the workplace, etc.

    Moderately critical: *May* contribute to improvement in public health, reduced crime, quality of life, safety at the workplace, etc.

    Not critical: *Probably would not* contribute to improvement in public health, reduced crime, quality of life, safety at the workplace, etc.

    Surplus (candidate for non-funding): *Will not* contribute to improvement in public health, reduced crime, quality of life, safety at the workplace, etc.

- Determine the relative urgency of each gap to establish a time schedule for dealing with the various needs that fall into the same priority levels determined by the criticality benchmarks listed earlier.

- Discuss your prioritized list of needs with your planning partners to make sure that everyone agrees with the needs, and their priority order. Make sure you reach group consensus on the needs, and the rationale for addressing them.

- Get your planning partners to commit to resolving the selected needs.

For example: *Fort Security prioritized its needs in terms of their perceived criticality. The planning partners at Fort Security decided that the following priority order was appropriate:*

Very critical:	*1.*	*Deaths due to terrorists.*
	2.	*The crime rate.*
	3.	*Incidents of discrimination.*
Moderately critical:	*4.*	*Improving self-sufficiency.*

A commitment was agreed upon, to address each of the above problems (needs) in the priority order indicated.

Step 4. Write a *realistic* mission objective which includes a specific sub-objective for each gap you decided to address (e.g., what you will have accomplished five or more years from now).

What is a *realistic* mission objective?

A realistic mission statement is one that specifies an achievable target accomplishment within a specific time. While your mission statement may be the same as your ideal vision, remember that your mission objective should be achievable within your target deadline.

Usually, a mission objective only takes on a part of the ideal vision—that part which it commits to contribute to. The *realistic* mission objective identifies how close to the ideal vision the organization will come in the future, for example in 10 years, three years, next year.

For example, STARBUCK Motor Company's mission objective (page 30) could use the ideal criteria and identify how close they will come by the year 2000 (e.g., emissions will not exceed air quality standards; there will be no more than one lawsuit judgement for poor/unsafe design, etc.).

Why write a mission objective?

While visions describe what we would like to accomplish *ideally,* a mission objective clearly specifies what we can accomplish *measurably* as we move systematically towards the ideal.

For example :   *The following is the Fort Security Company's Mega-level mission objective:*

"By December 31, 199X the Fort Security Company's safety records will be perfect, as indicated by no fatalities or injuries due to terrorist activities in any airport where Fort is in charge of security operations."

"To accomplish our mission, we will achieve an improvement of 2% in our performance records on both simulated and real terrorist incidents, every year for the next 5 years, so that we will progressively work towards accomplishing our mission by our target deadline."

Figure 2.4 illustrates Fort Security's annual progression plan for accomplishing the company's mission. Note that the 199X objective is the same as the mission objective. Also note that the accomplishments of each year build on the accomplishments of the previous year(s).

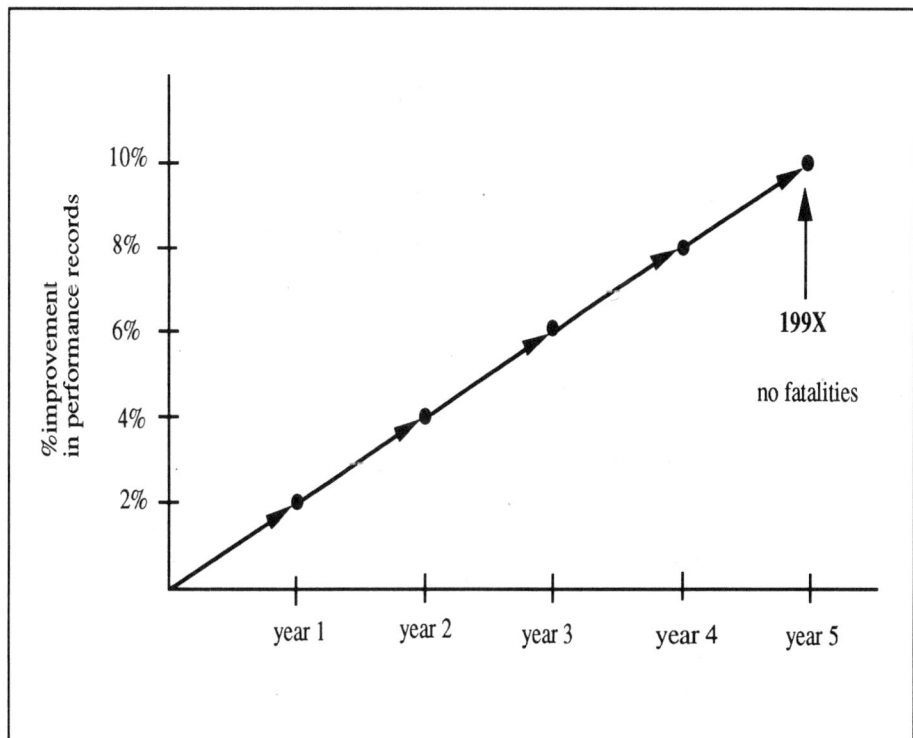

Figure 2.4. Fort Security's annual progression plan for accomplishing the company's mission.

Step 5. Break down your mission objective to functional building-block objectives.

What are building-block objectives?

Building-block objectives are the elements of your mission objective that you can accomplish as the focus (target) of your organization's business plan. In a Mega-level needs assessment, your building-block objectives will be at the Macro level—Outputs and the Micro levels—Products. When accomplished, your building-block objectives will deliver the required Mega-level results, and thus accomplish the mission objective.

For example: *Some of the building-block—non-Mega-level—objectives for the Fort Security Company are:*

- *All security guards will be able to demonstrate the skills required to intercept any real and/or simulated terrorist attacks successfully.*
- *All passengers, traveling through airports where Fort Security is in charge, will be satisfied with the quality and thoroughness of security checks, and with the manner in which such checks are carried out.*
- *Airport and airline personnel will provide any necessary assistance to Fort Security staff and cooperate at all times to ensure that Fort Security can carry out its responsibilities as required.*
- *There will be no complaints or security breaks.*

Why have building-block objectives?

Building-block objectives serve three major purposes:

1. They help you work progressively towards accomplishing your mission objective (and the ideal vision), thus ensuring that your organization operates cohesively towards a common and useful destination.
2. They help you to determine levels of responsibility for addressing each building-block objective, depending on whether it is at the Mega, Macro, or Micro level.
3. They provide the criteria for:

- Detailed planning objectives.
- Identifying and selecting the ways and means to meet the objectives.
- Evaluating progress and accomplishment.
- Knowing what to fix and why.

For example: *Figure 2.5 shows how integration of the ideal vision, organizational mission, and building-block objectives might be achieved.*

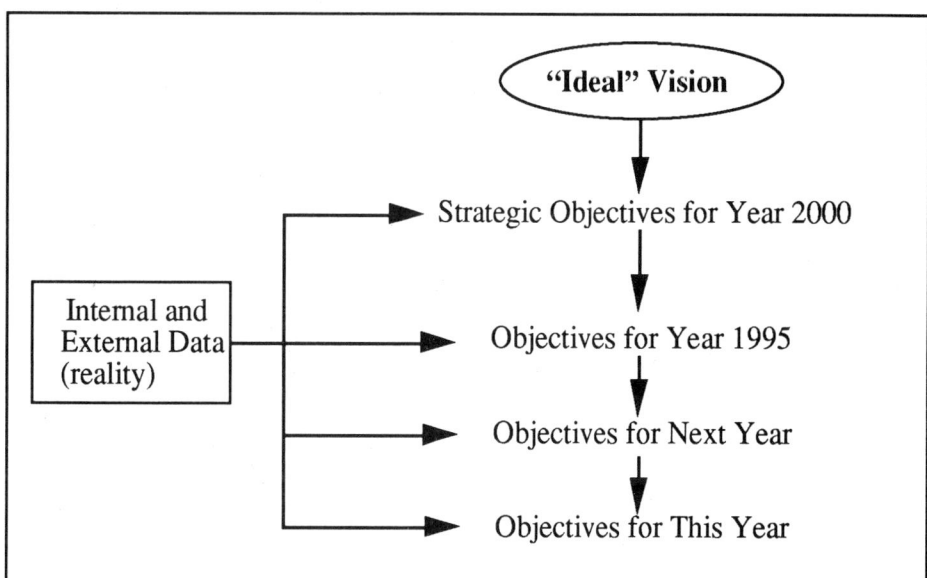

Figure 2.5. Relating the ideal vision to building-block objectives. (Based on Kaufman & Herman, 1991. With permission.)

Referring to the Organizational Elements Model (Figure 1.5), all elements should be mutually contributing to what organizations use (inputs), do (processes), develop (products), deliver (outputs), and contribute to external clients and society (outcomes). You will also improve the usefulness of what you use, do, and deliver.

Guidelines for setting building-block objectives:

- In your meeting with your planning partners, guide the group through determining building-block objectives. Assure they are results-based.
- Determine the level for each building-block objective. (Note that because your organizational mission is derived from an ideal societal vision, your building-block objectives will be in both the Macro and Micro levels.)

- Assign roles and responsibilities for the accomplishment of each functional objective.
- Elect a "Needs Assessment Project Alignment Coordinator." This person's role will be to ensure organizational cohesiveness and focus on the mission.

Step 6. Present your Mega-level needs to your clients for concurrence.

Who are your clients?

Your actual clients include all your stakeholders. Your planning partners are representatives of your stakeholders' various constituencies—e.g., representatives of your organization's executive officers, your clients, employees/associates, your potential clients, society, and community representatives.

Why is client concurrence required?

Client concurrence is important in order to:

- Make certain that no needs have been overlooked.
- Obtain commitment and joint ownership by organizational and community leaders who will help in the implementation of plans to address identified needs.
- Prevent resistance from anyone who might potentially block the implementation of plans to address identified needs.

How to present Mega-level needs to your client

Present the Mega-level needs (agreed upon by your planning partners) to your clients by using a needs assessment summary form, such as the one shown in Table 2.4.

For example: Table 2.4 presents the Mega-level Needs Assessment Summary Form prepared for the Fort Security Company.

MEGA-LEVEL NEEDS ASSESSMENT—CHAPTER 2

NEEDS	*PRIORITY*
• **Deaths due to terrorists** should be prevented by next year (there were 13 deaths this year).	1
• **The crime rate** in our community (currently 57 reported incidents) should be eliminated within the next five years.	2
• **Incidents of discrimination** (23 reported this year) because of color, gender, age, religion, or national origin should be eliminated within the next five years.	3
• The 8% of our society who are on welfare or otherwise **not self-sufficient** will all be able to care for themselves (i.e., become self-sufficient) within the next ten years.	4

Table 2.4. A hypothetical Mega-level Needs Assessment Summary Form.

A blank Needs Assessment Summary Form is provided at the end of this chapter (see Form 2.3). Use this form to present Mega-level needs to your own clients.

Step 7. Identify and list alternative methods and means for addressing your Mega-level need(s), and identify the advantages and disadvantages of each.

What are methods and means?

Methods are procedures and techniques we use to address needs. Examples of methods may include:

- Training.
- Team building.
- Managing by objectives.
- Tactical planning.
- Strategic planning.
- Recruiting.
- Operating.
- Economic analysis.

Means are tools and resources we use to address needs. Examples of means may include:

- Books.
- Fork lift trucks.
- Money.
- Computers.
- Surgical tools.
- Personnel.

Why list alternative methods and means?

To identify the various possible resources, tools, and ways by which your objectives and mission can be accomplished, and to determine the advantages and disadvantages of each alternative.

Once the advantages and disadvantages of alternative methods and means have been identified, you will be ready to select the appropriate methods and means to meet your needs, implement your plans, and revise as and when required.

How to identify methods-means

Chapter 5 in this book provides an outline of the steps and procedures to take when you are identifying the methods and means required to meet your needs.

Chapter Summary

Needs assessments identify gaps between current results and desired ones, and place those gaps in priority order. Priority may be set by asking planning partners to rank order the needs on the basis of "what it costs to meet the need" versus "what it costs to ignore the need."

In this chapter we defined Mega-level Needs Assessment and explained when and how to do it. The key points of this chapter are listed below:

- Mega-level Needs Assessment is the process of identifying and resolving the gaps between the actual and the desired accomplishments of an organization as measured by the *usefulness* of these accomplishments to the organization's external clients and society.
- Mega-level Needs Assessment should be the mandatory approach of any organization that impacts external clients and society.
- The seven major steps for conducting a Mega-level Needs Assessment include:

    1. Determine your organization's **ideal vision**, including indicators of its impact on the survival and quality of life of its external clients and society.

2. Determine your organization's **current status** with regard to its impact on clients' and society's survival and quality of life.
3. Place Mega-level gaps (i.e., Needs) between your ideal vision and the current status, in a priority order, based on the cost to ignore vs. the cost to successfully address each identified need.
4. Write a *realistic* mission objective which includes a specific sub-objective for each gap you decided to address (e.g., what you will have accomplished five or more years from now).
5. Break down your mission objective to functional building-block objectives.
6. Present your Mega-level needs to your clients for concurrence.
7. Identify and list alternative methods and means for addressing your Mega-level need(s) and identify the advantages and disadvantages of each.

References and Suggested Readings

Drucker, P. F. (1973) *Management: Tasks, responsibilities, practices.* New York: Harper & Row.

Drucker, P. F. (1992, Sept.-Oct.) The new society of organizations, *Harvard Business Review.*

Kanter, R. M. (1989) *When giants learn to dance: Mastering the challenges of strategy, management, and careers in the 1990's.* New York: Simon & Schuster.

Kaufman, R. (1988, Sept.) Preparing useful performance indicators. *Training & Development Journal.*

Kaufman, R. (1992a) *Strategic planning plus: An organizational guide.* Newbury Park, CA: Sage Publishing.

Kaufman, R. (1992b) *Mapping educational success.* Newbury Park, CA: Corwin Press, Division of Sage.

Kaufman, R. & Herman, J. (1991) *Strategic planning in education: Rethinking, restructuring, revitalizing.* Lancaster, PA: Technomic Publishing Co.

Kaufman, R. & Rojas, A. (1985) *Needs assessment.* Tallahassee, FL: Florida State Department of Health & Rehabilitative Services and the Center for Needs Assessment & Planning.

Mager, R. F. (1975) *Preparing instructional objectives* (2nd Ed.). Belmont, CA: David S. Lake Publishers.

Peters, T. (1987) *Thriving on chaos: Handbook for a management revolution.* New York: Alfred A. Knopf.

Rummler, G. A. & Brache, A. P. (1990) *Improving performance: How to manage the white space on the organization chart.* San Francisco, CA: Jossey-Bass.

Senge, P. M. (1990) *The fifth discipline: The art and practice of the learning organization.* New York: Doubleday.

Endnote:

[1] Recall that an organization will not be responsible for all elements of the ideal vision. The organization's mission simply identifies those ideal vision elements for which it will be accountable. Thus, on pages 32, 35, and 37, the 8% non-self sufficient rate might be eliminated from the mission objective or it might form a part of an outreach program the organization chooses to pursue.

Forms

Ideal Vision	Results Criteria

Form 2.1. A form for listing your ideal vision and results criteria.

Ideal Vision	Current Status

Form 2.2. A form for deriving current status of variables included in an ideal vision.

Mega Need(s)	Priority

Form 2.3. A Mega-level Needs Assessment form.

MACRO-LEVEL NEEDS ASSESSMENT

Chapter 3

Key points:

- What is Macro-level Needs Assessment?

- When and why do a Macro-level Needs Assessment.

- Payoffs and consequences of conducting a Macro-level Needs Assessment linked to a Mega-level Needs Assessment.

- The relationship between Total Quality Management and needs assessment at the Mega and Macro levels.

- The tools, techniques, and steps to use to conduct a Macro-level Needs Assessment.

Macro-Level Needs Assessment—Chapter 3

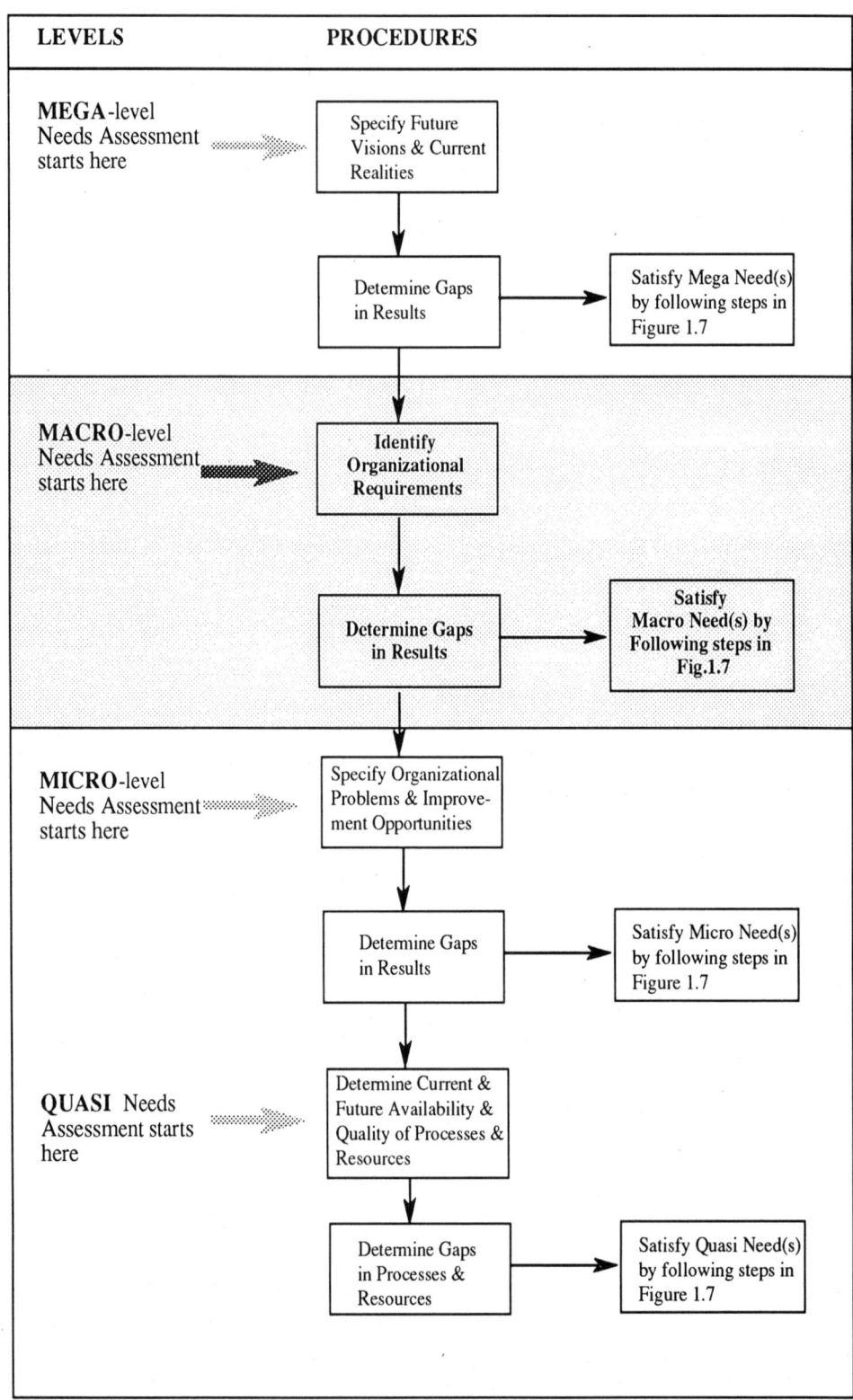

A guide to follow when conducting needs assessment at Mega, Macro, and Micro levels, and when identifying Quasi Needs. The shaded area focuses on information in this chapter.

*Consider the
following
likely scenario:* You are the internal consultant for the Product Training Support Group of Elitech—a high-tech company. The manager of sales and marketing at Elitech indicates to you that even though sales have been up during the last quarter, there is a concern regarding customer satisfaction. It seems that the support given to customers is not adequate for an effective and efficient utilization of a laser printer recently released. During weekly meetings your group discusses the best ways to improve customer satisfaction. Many solutions are presented. Some of your colleagues are concerned about the quality of the training delivered; others think that the printer itself has some inefficient features. The company executives are interested in the continuing growth of sales as well as in maintaining a high level of customer satisfaction. Your manager requests that you prepare a brief proposal in which you should outline your strategy for identifying customers' needs and wants. The intention is that the identified needs would provide the company with a focus and a target for improving the quality of products, as measured by customer satisfaction.

What would you do?

The competition for quality products as well as high levels of customer satisfaction are the focus of modern companies, so they label such efforts "Total Quality Management" (TQM) and "continuous improvement." However, this type of industry is not the only one interested in the quality of what they deliver to external clients. Such concerns are showed by business, industry, health organizations, and public education. By using the appropriate needs assessment approach, you will be able to satisfy customers' needs (and wants) by offering the best solution based on documented gaps in results.

The type of needs assessment that you should conduct to respond to our scenario is a **Macro-level Needs Assessment**, the topic of this chapter.

What is Macro-level Needs Assessment?

Macro-level Needs Assessment is a process for identifying and resolving gaps between the actual and the desired quality of what your organization delivers to external clients (Kaufman, 1992a, b).

Macro-Level Needs Assessment—Chapter 3

For example: Macro-level Needs Assessment may measure the difference between the desired and current results of:

- Sales of automobiles.
- Number of patients discharged from a hospital.
- Quality and/or quantity of printers delivered to the market.
- Quality and number of certified trainers—the trainers who will train other people using the training package of your company.

In the case of Elitech, the organization is interested in improving the quality of its products, as measured by customer satisfaction. Elitech is focusing on addressing its needs at the **Macro level.**

The process of needs assessment at the Macro level is illustrated in Figure 3.1.

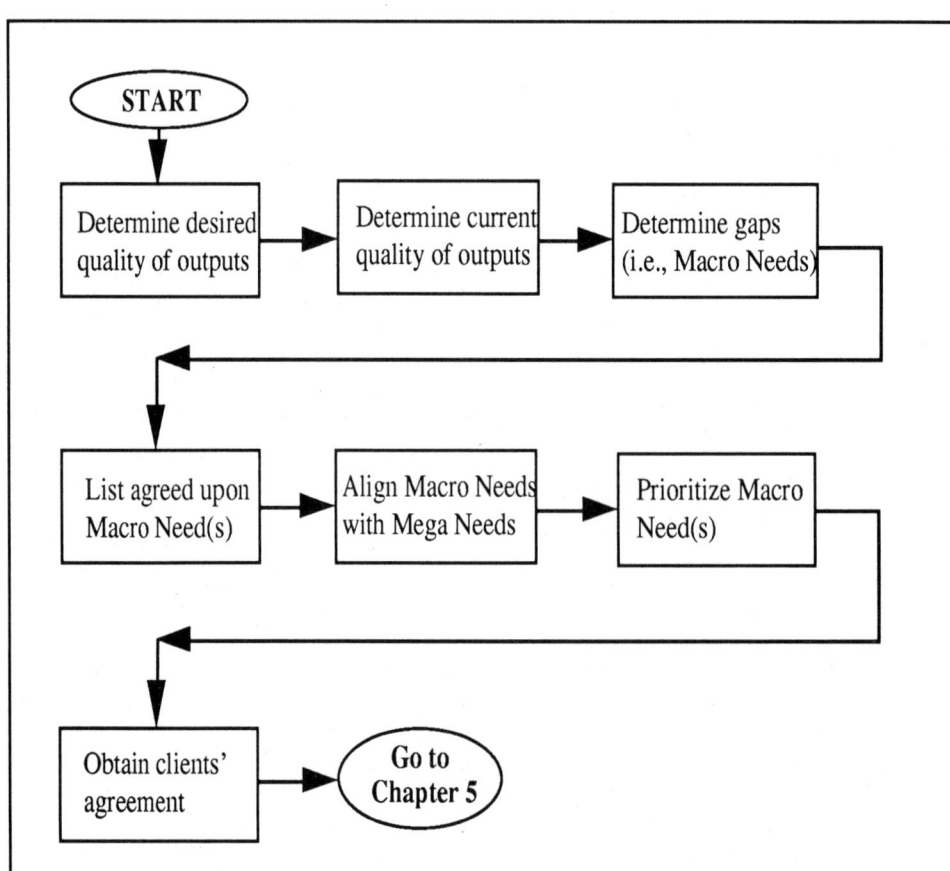

Figure 3.1. Macro-level Needs Assessment functions.

When and why should a Macro-level Needs Assessment be done?

We have already discussed that there are several types of needs assessment, based on the scope selected for planning: Mega, Macro, and Micro levels.

The selection of one of the types of planning and needs assessment, either formally or by assumption, will determine the nature of the organization's "vision" and the starting place for needs assessment and planning. A macro variety will regard the company itself as the primary stakeholder and beneficiary. Whenever an organization is concerned with quality in terms of client *satisfaction* (or market share or quarterly sales) of *what gets delivered* outside the organization, a Macro-level Needs Assessment is appropriate.

Thus, when an organization and its needs assessment partners decide to conduct a needs assessment at the Macro level, it means that the organization is concerned with closing the gaps in results related to the quality of what gets delivered and what should be delivered outside the organization to external clients. It *does not* consider the usefulness of the output.

For example: *Elitech wants to determine if customer satisfaction can be improved regarding the complaints received about the quality of the product delivered: a laser printer.*

Do note, however, that a Macro-level Needs Assessment is most appropriate *after* a Mega-level Needs Assessment has been carried out (see Chapter 2). Remember that ultimately, the quality of what your organization delivers to its clients is a function of its usefulness and appeal.

For example: *The local post office branch has been flooded with complaints about the quality of its services. In fact, some people have chosen to get a post office box in a neighboring county, and get their mail delivered there, rather than put up with the poor quality of the postal service. As a result, the post office branch has lost some of its business to competitors (e.g., courier services, postal services in neighboring counties, fax services). The post office branch is determined to improve the quality of its services and reduce customer complaints. The manager in charge decided to adopt a Macro-level approach to assessing the company's needs: the required quality of the services delivered in order to improve customer satisfaction.*

Client-Centered Actions. A subtle-but-important characteristic of the Macro-level approach is that it targets organizational contributions to external client's *satisfaction only.*

Recognition of the centrality of the client has become both fashionable and profitable (Bennis & Nannus, 1985; Kanter, 1989; Kaufman, 1990; 1992a, b; Peters, 1987). Several giant firms are now viewing their salvation in becoming **market-driven** by being customer-oriented and are hurrying off to be the best at that—whatever that means. Market-driven approaches, interpreted and interpretable in multiple ways, intend to show the way to responsiveness and profits by being client-responsive. The market resides with the client, and s/he has to be satisfied and happy...find out what the client wants and what s/he can use and make it available. Synergy comes from combining forces to leverage far-flung resources to be responsive to the changing—often seemingly chaotic—marketplace (Kanter, 1989). "Quality" seeks to have everyone in the synergistic organization become partners in delivering outputs (deliverables) that they themselves would want to buy.

Being market-driven means understanding the importance of the client for one's continuing success. Market-driven people generally ask:

- What do you want?
- What are your requirements?
- What can you pay?
- What can you afford?
- Will it work?
- Do you think what we have will help you?
- What barriers (problems) exist which prevent or inhibit sales?

More and more organizations are discovering the wisdom of being client-oriented. But is this enough? While a client might be satisfied with something we deliver, it might not "work" for them. For example, what if it pollutes? What if it is dangerous and a threat to our well-being, health, and/or life? Have you ever bought something which was not good for you? Harmful to the environment? Our ultimate target should be to be both satisfied with what we purchase and receive *and* happy with its impact on our quality of life. This is the topic and focus of Mega-level Needs Assessment and planning, covered in Chapter 2.

Marketing, by its usual definition, is **reactive**—you go out and find what clients want and provide it. But why limit one's potential contribution to *reacting* to potential clients' missions (or their market plans) and not to develop a **proactive** identification of what customers, our nation, and the world should and could use in the future?

Finding the common ground of mutual interest and payoffs (among ourselves, the external client, and the world) will be more successful. The mutual interest questions—the road less traveled—will include the market-driven questions (Macro-level scope) **plus** (Mega-level scope):

- What barriers (problems) exist which prevent or inhibit our mutual progress (or growth)?
- What do your clients' clients require?
- What is good for you, us, and the world?
- What do I have which meets our shared requirements?
- What can others supply which might be better and/or more useful than what I have?
- Does everyone benefit, now, and in the future?
- What might be created, or invented, which will be responsive to future opportunities or problems?

We therefore suggest, again, that you apply a **proactive** approach to the conduct of needs assessment. You should start by focusing on the Mega level rather than beginning at the Macro level of needs assessment (Kaufman, Stith, & Kaufman, 1992). The choice, of course, is yours.

Total Quality Management and Needs Assessment

Quality means **doing it right the first time, and every time**. Total quality management is an organization's systemic, strong commitment to quality at all levels, all functions, and at all times (Crosby, 1986; Deal, 1991). The press for "total quality" is strong and sensible. Applications in Japan (the famous Deming Awards) and in the U.S. (the Department of Commerce's Malcolm Baldridge Award) are organizational initiatives to "do it right the first time." American corporations and organizations are scrambling to pick up the coveted award (cf. DeYoung, 1990) and/or complying with ISO 9000. Given the emergence of global competitiveness, the incentives are vital, and timely.

While the criteria for winning a total quality award vary (Bhote, 1989) from very specific (the Baldridge Award) to relatively non-specific (the Deming Awards), each seems to target the same areas: customer satisfaction, quality output, quality products and components, worker competence and concern, quality inputs, procedures, and resources.

Do most total quality programs go far enough? Based on the Organizational Elements Model (Chapter 1), and the scope of a Mega-level approach (Chapter 2) versus a Macro-level approach (Chapter 3), total quality approaches focus primarily on the Macro-level, and therefore cover *only part* of the mega/outcomes level: client satisfaction (Kaufman, 1990, 1991).

Of course, satisfied clients are crucial to a viable business. But is that enough? Isn't there more? Figure 3.2 shows how typical total quality program elements relate to each other. The elements generally "roll-up" from quality resources and inputs to processes (where workers care about what gets produced for the client), to quality products and components, to the outputs—i.e., what gets delivered to the client. Client satisfaction is the result of "doing it right the first time and every time" at each element along the "rolling-up" process. The basic driving force behind being "market-driven" is, therefore, a **reaction** to market demands and client requests.

But what about the contributions and usefulness of that which satisfies the clients? We can think of many client-pleasing things which might not be helpful or even safe in the long run. A few items which have resulted in client satisfaction and high sales (and profits) which turned out to be unacceptable (if not downright unhealthy) include:

Plastic bags (non-biodegradable)	DDT
Styrofoam cups/packaging/utensils	Chlordane (for red ants)
Well-marbled beef	Leaf blowers
Cigarettes/tobacco products	Chicken with skin
Disposable diapers	Alar
Aerosol/fluorocarbon sprays	Newspaper ink
Asbestos	Leaded gasoline
Electric blankets	Freon
Suntans	Loud rock music

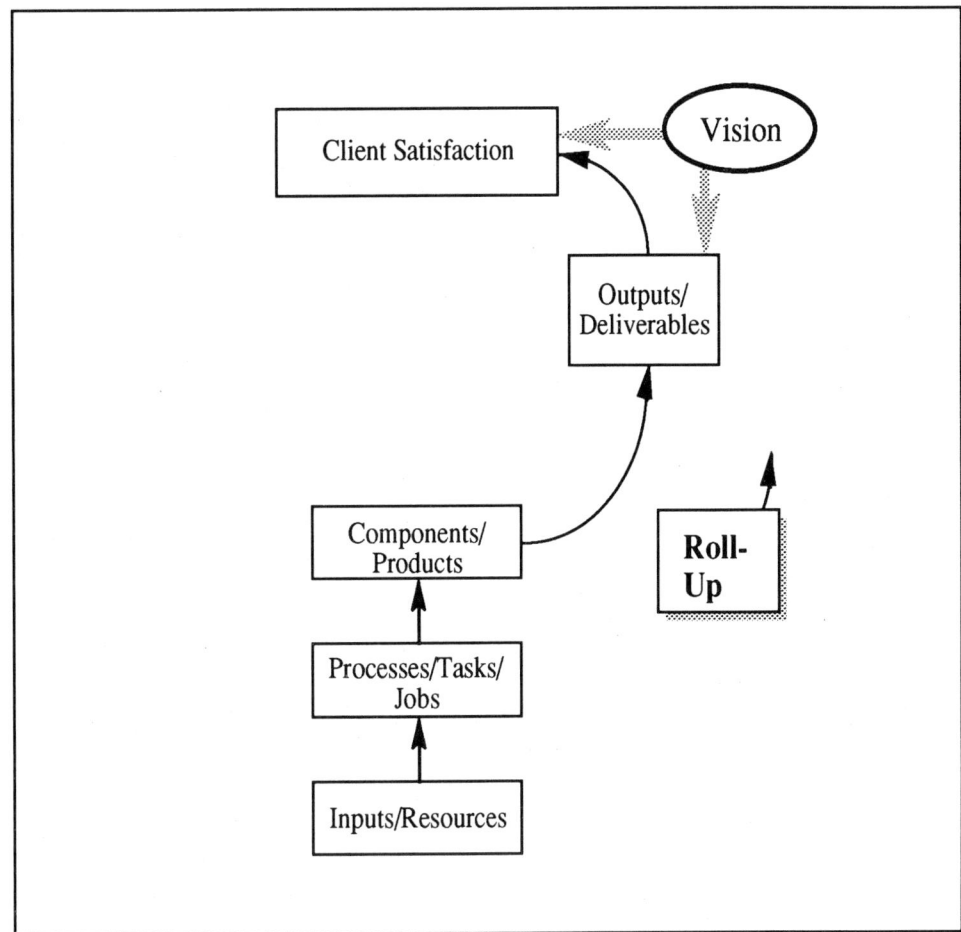

Figure 3.2. The linked (rolled-up) elements in a usual "total quality management" program. (Based on Kaufman, 1991.)

Total Quality Management Plus and Needs Assessment

Each of the above items (you can probably add to the list) could be the subject of a total quality management program. Each would result in client satisfaction; but none would bring about total quality *usefulness* (to the client and our shared world). Figure 3.3 provides a *total quality management plus* framework, which rolls down from societal usefulness (the **Mega level**), to define that which should be delivered to the client.

The integrated roll-up and roll-down approach is shown in Figure 3.4. The roll-down process with the roll-up contributions of conventional total quality management provide a focus on the importance of both client satisfaction and societal usefulness. *Total quality management plus*

Macro-Level Needs Assessment—Chapter 3

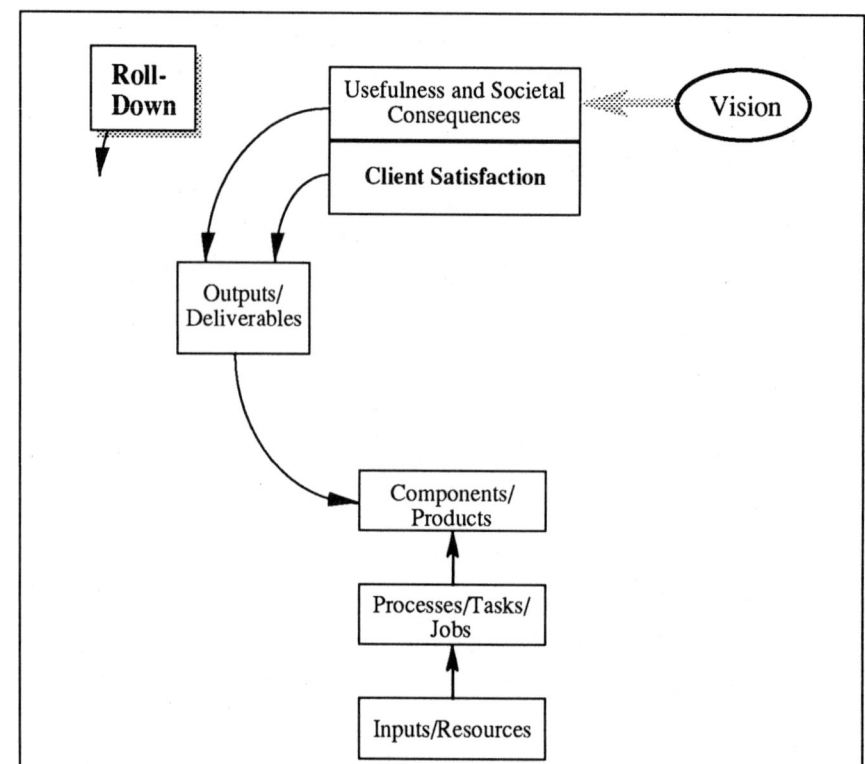

Figure 3.3. Total quality management plus elements and their roll-down sequence (Kaufman, 1991).

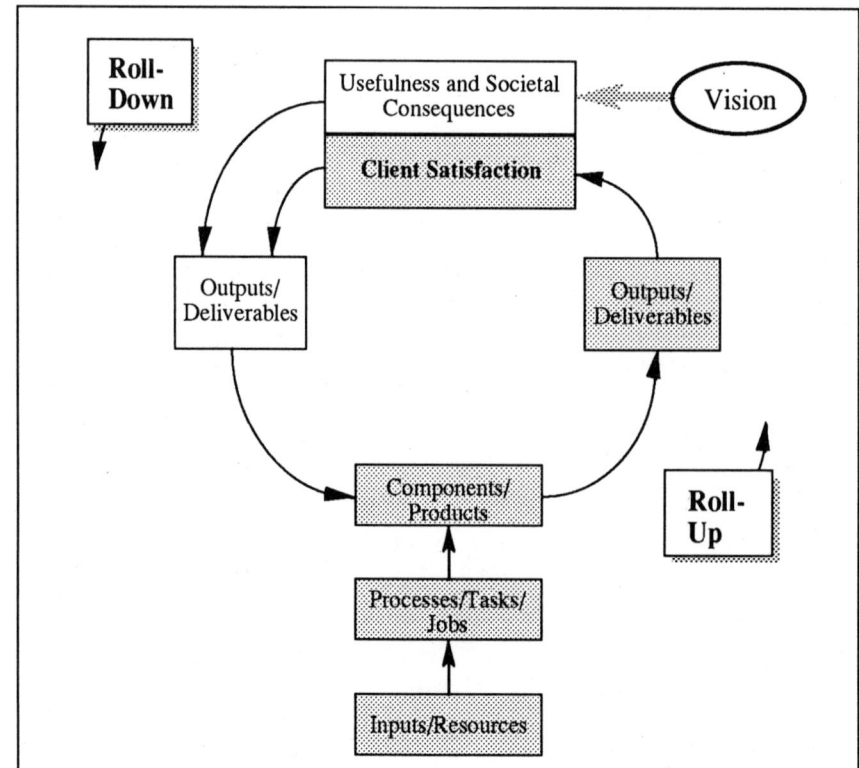

Figure 3.4. The components of total quality management plus. The first element is determining what would create a better world as well as client satisfaction. It then rolls down from there until it meets with a conventional total quality management roll-up cycle (Kaufman, 1991).

(Kaufman, 1991) is therefore a process that takes conventional total quality management an important step further; it takes a good idea and extends it meaningfully.

Note: *"Total quality management plus"—related assessment properly belongs in the chapter on Mega-level Needs Assessment. Because most conventional total quality management programs are focused at the Macro level, the entire topic is presented here.*

How to do a Macro-level Needs Assessment

The scope of needs assessment at the Macro level requires that attention be given to the quality of an organization's outputs, as measured by external client satisfaction.

The following are the specific steps and procedures for doing a Macro-level Needs Assessment.

Step 1. Determine the desired quality of what your organization delivers to external clients.

The desired quality of a company's outputs (Macro-level deliverables) can be measured in terms of external client satisification. Organizations generally envision their ideally desired quality in terms of the perfect output or service they want to deliver.

For example: *Elitech's (see scenario at the beginning of this chapter) vision of the desired quality of its deliverables may be:*

- *All laser printers will be delivered to clients with 0 defects.*
- *There will be 0 complaints regarding the laser printer's performance.*
- *There will be 100% customer satisifaction as indicated by customer surveys.*
- *There will be 0 warranty work.*
- *The laser printer sales will account for 80% of the total market share.*
- *The printer will be known as having the best price, the highest prestige, and the fastest customer service.*

Note that the desired quality may not necessarily be the ideal vision of perfection. It can also be defined as what the company can and wants to deliver, realistically, say in the next 2 years (while keeping in mind the desired vision of perfection).

For example: *In our scenario with Elitech, the company has already determined that its output (i.e., a high-resolution laser printer) will represent the state-of-the-art in laser printers; it will cost 5% less than the top of the line printer available in the market; there will be no more than 2% warranty requests during the first year; the printer will function very quietly; and it will print 10% more pages per minute than the closest competitor in the market.*

How to determine the desired quality of your organization's output

The organization may define the desired quality of its deliverables by responding to market requirements. In order to specify the desired quality, several partners may participate in the process, such as customers, employees, and representatives of the public at large.

Data (facts and perceptions—*hard* and *soft* data) must be collected to determine the quality criteria and standards expected for these deliverables.

The *hard data (independently verifiable facts and figures)* are provided by the company's performance indicators. Some of these indicators may include:

- Sales.
- Levels of complaints about tardiness of deliver.
- Service requests at various center.
- Toll-free customer service lines data.
- Accepted deliveries of goods and services.

Human partners provide the *soft data (personal perceptions)* such as:

- Values.
- Beliefs.
- Opinions.
- Visions.
- Perceived needs.

Some sources for Macro-level (*hard* and *soft*) data may include:

- Customer surveys.
- Market analyses.
- Company standards for its outputs.
- Legislation on standards, where applicable.
- Strategic plans of the company.
- Field testing data.
- Customer comments, complaints, suggestions.

Guidelines for determining the desired quality of your organization's output (Macro-level results):

- Determine the appropriate data sources for each output area.
- Obtain the necessary hard and soft data for each output area.
- Present the data you collected on the desired quality of your organization's output to your group of planning partners (e.g., managers, marketing department, associates, external clients, etc.).
- Identify agreements and disagreements among your planning partners regarding the desired quality of each output area.
- Reconcile any disagreements among your planning partners and reach consensus on the desired output for each deliverable area.
- State the desired quality of your organization's output.

Step 2. Determine the current quality of what your organization delivers to external clients.

The current status of the same variables you included in Step 1 ("Determine the desired quality...") should include a description of both the type and extent of your Macro-level accomplishments.

This step is crucial to:

- Determine any gaps between the organization's desired and current accomplishments that the organization must resolve in order to successfully accomplish its Macro-level vision.
- Make certain that the current accomplishments meeting the desired quality criteria and standards are maintained and will continue to be delivered without any changes...keep what is working, and change what isn't.

How to determine the current status

Data (facts and perceptions—*hard* and *soft* data) must be collected to determine the current status of the organization's deliverables.

Some sources of Macro-level *(hard* and *soft)* data on the *current* status of deliverables may include:

- Customer feedback.
- Products returned for malfunctioning.
- Dealer complaints.
- Reports on repairs.
- Newspaper and trade journal/magazine reports.
- Sales documents.
- Field tests.

For example: Continuing with our scenario...according to customers' feedback, Elitech's printer is not performing to the standards specified in the advertising and technical manual. A table was completed as a follow-up to identify the current quality of the organization's output as indicated by several sources (Table 3.1).

Current status of the output	Sources
Prints same amount of pages per minute as competitor's printer.	Customers and service person field test data (*)
Costs 2.5% less than the top of the line printer available in the market.	Marketing analysis Trade journal reports and surveys (*)
Performs very quietly.	User field test data (*)
3% warranty returns requested during the first 6 months. (**)	Product support monthly report (*)
It is a state-of-the-art model.	Newspaper review and technical magazines–may include soft and hard data

Table 3.1. Current quality of the organization's output as indicated by several sources.

*Hard data   **Actually at the Mega-level due to use in the client's environment

Macro-Level Needs Assessment—Chapter 3

Guidelines for determining the current status of your organization's output:

- Determine the appropriate data sources for each output area.
- Obtain the necessary hard and soft data for each output area.
- Present current status data to your group of planning partners (e.g., managers, marketing department, associates, external clients, etc.). You may complete the form provided at the end of this chapter (Form 3.1) Use the completed form as a basis for the planning partners' group discussion.
- Identify agreements and disagreements among your planning partners regarding the status of each output area.
- State the current status data by recording the findings.

Step 3. List the identified, agreed upon need(s).

Any discrepancy between the desired quality of the organization's output and its current status is a Macro-level need (see Figure 3.5).

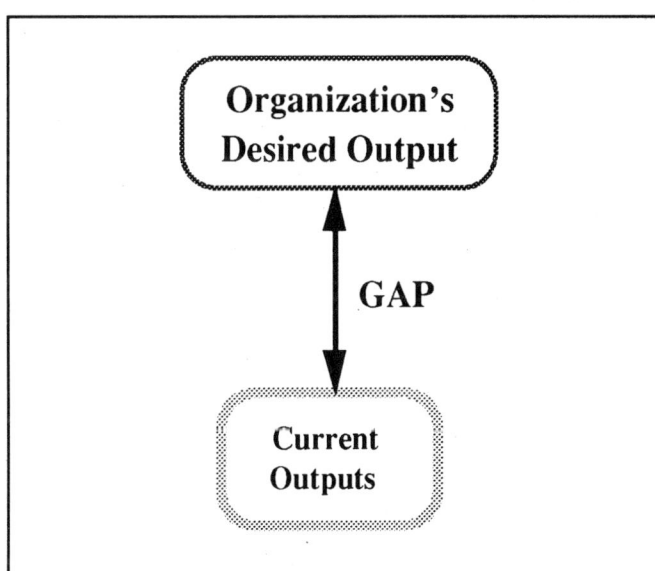

Figure 3.5. Discrepancy between the desired quality of the organization's output and its current status.

For example: Continuing with our example... A table such as Table 3.2 can be completed to identify the gaps (needs), if there are any, between the desired and current quality of Elitech's output.

Table 3.2. Determination of needs.

Current status of the output	Desired quality	Need
Prints same amount of pages as competitor's printer.	Prints same amount of pages as competitor's printer.	No discrepancy.
Costs 2.5% less than the top of the line printer available in the market.	Costs 5% less than the top of the line printer available in the market.	2.5% price differential.
Performs very quietly.	Performs very quietly.	No discrepancy.
3% warranty returns during the first 6 months.(*)	2% warranty returns during the first 6 months.(*)	1% discrepancy warranty.
It is an example of the state-of-the-art of the technology.	It is an example of the state-of-the-art of the technology.	No discrepancy.
Most businesses prefer this printer. Public agencies do not like it that much.	Prefered as "the" printer for all types of businesses including public sector agencies.	Gap in customers' perceptions.

*Actually at the Mega level due to use in the client's environment

Complete Form 3.2 (provided at the end of this chapter) and present it in your meeting with your planning partners. Reach agreement with the planning partners on the identified needs you listed.

Step 4. Align the needs identified at the Macro level with the vision and mission of your organization.

It is vital that the needs do align with the mission and vision. This step seeks to assure the linkages.

For example: *In the case of Elitech, customer satisfaction is lower than desired because the price is not as low as promised, and the requirement for services during the warranty period (and beyond) is higher than expected. Elitech is interested in improving customer satisfaction. The company believes that this can best be accomplished by implementing policies that reflect Elitech's Mega-level vision and mission: For instance, it is the company's goal to produce printers that will function properly and use paper efficiently (and will also be cost-competitive and function properly). Then customer satisfaction will be improved and aligned with the company's Mega-level vision and mission–because of lower paper wastage. Elitech must find a way to improve the quality of its printers so that environment friendly printers are also cost-competitive and function properly. Then customer satisfaction will be improved and aligned with the company's Mega-level vision and mission.*

Step 5. Place Macro-level needs in a priority order, based on the cost to ignore versus the cost to address each identified need.

- Present current status data to your group of planning partners (e.g., managers, marketing department, associates, external clients, etc.). You may complete the form provided at the end of this chapter (Form 3.1). Use the completed form as a basis for the planning partners' group discussion.
- Identify agreements and disagreements among your planning partners regarding the status of each output area.
- Reconcile any disagreements among your planning partners and reach consensus for each deliverable area.
- State the current status data by recording the findings.

Guidelines for prioritizing Macro-level needs:

- Answer the following questions:
  - What will it **cost to meet** the need?
  - What will it **cost to ignore** the need?

If it will cost you more to meet the need than to ignore it, you should ignore it.

Note: "Cost" as used here relates not only to immediate dollar outlay but also to costs in terms of future money outlays, resources, and other intangibles such as image, social good, opportunity lost, marketability, and future organizational survival and contributions.

- Determine the criteria to be used for prioritizing needs. Be sure that the criteria are consistent with your organization's vision and mission.

- Use the prioritizing method that is most appropriate for your company. There are several ways to prioritize needs. One is to sort the identified needs into categories that fit your situation. For instance, the categories might be:

  ____ **Critical** (must be resolved within the next 6 months).
  ____ **Very important** (must be resolved within the next year).
  ____ **Important** (should be resolved within 2 years).
  ____ **Minimal** (should be dealt with, but only if enough time and resources are left over from higher priority needs).
  ____ **Not important** (not necessary to deal with).
  ____ **Not a need** (Yes! You and the group may discover that a "need" was wrongly stated as such!).

For example: *In our scenario...Two of the needs to be resolved at Elitech are: discrepancy of 2.5% in the price; 1% discrepancy in the percent of requests for service received while printers are still under warranty. Several criteria were used to determine the importance of resolving one before others. Again, the decision was also linked to the vision of the company. The planning group (marketing, sales, research and development, and training) considered both needs critical for the company to reach the quality desired and to continue to have the reputation of the best company on the market in terms of responsiveness to customer feedback. They agreed to address both needs within the next six months.*

Step 6. Present your Macro-level needs to your clients for concurrence.

Who are your clients?

Your clients include all your stakeholders, e.g., your external clients (who buy your deliverables/outputs), your potential clients (who may buy your deliverables/outputs), all your company's executive officers, and employees/associates.

Why is client concurrence required?

Client concurrence is important in order to:

- Make certain that no needs have been overlooked.
- Obtain commitment and joint ownership of organizational and major client group leaders who will help in the implementation of plans to address identified needs.
- Prevent and/or overcome resistance from anyone who might potentially block the implementation of plans to address identified needs.

How to present Macro-level needs to your clients

Present the Macro-level needs (agreed upon by your planning partners) to your clients by using a needs assessment summary form, such as the one shown in Table 3.3.

A blank Needs Assessment Summary Form is provided at the end of this chapter (see Form 3.3). Use this form to present Macro-level needs to your own clients.

For example: *Table 3.3 presents the Macro Needs Assessment Summary Form prepared for the Elitech Company.*

Table 3.3. Macro-level needs summary.

NEEDS	Priority
1. Discrepancy of 2.5% in the printer price	CRITICAL
2. 1% discrepancy in the percent of request for service	CRITICAL

Step 7. List alternative methods and means for addressing your Macro-level need(s), and identify the advantages and disadvantages of each.

Chapter 5 in this book provides an outline of the steps and procedures to take when you are identifying the various methods and means you may require to meet your needs.

Chapter Summary

By using the appropriate needs assessment approach, you will be able to identify and satisfy customers' needs (not just wants) by offering the best solution based on documented needs.

The selection of one of the types of planning and needs assessment, either formally or by assumption, will determine the nature of the organization's "vision" and the starting place for needs assessment and planning. A Macro-level Needs Assessment will regard the company as the primary stakeholder and beneficiary. Whenever an organization is concerned with the quality of what gets delivered outside the organization, a Macro-level Needs Assessment is appropriate.

Macro-level Needs Assessment is a process for identifying and resolving gaps between the actual and the desired quality of what your organization delivers to external clients. The model used to conduct a needs assessment at the Macro level is the same as the model used for other levels. The difference will be in the scope of the process.

In this chapter, we defined Macro-level Needs Assessment and explained when, why, and how to do it (i.e., when the primary client and beneficiary is the organization itself).

The steps to use when conducting a Macro-level Needs Assessment are:

1. Determine the desired quality of what your organization delivers to external clients.
2. Determine the current quality of what your organization delivers to external clients.
3. List the identified, agreed upon need(s).
4. Align the needs identified at the Macro level with the vision and mission of your organization.
5. Place Macro-level needs in a priority order, based on the cost to ignore versus the cost to address each identified need.
6. Present your Macro-level needs to your clients for concurrence.
7. Identify and list alternative methods and means for addressing your Macro-level need(s) and identify the advantages and disadvantages of each.

References and Suggested Readings

Bennis, W. & Nannus, B. (1985) *Leaders: The strategies for taking charge.* New York: Harper & Row.

Bhote, K. R. (1989, Autumn) The Malcolm Baldridge Quality Award. *National Productivity Review, Vol. 8, No. 4.*

Crosby, P. B. (1986) *Quality without tears: The art of hassle-free management.* New York: New American Library.

Deal, T. F. (1991) *Developing a quality culture.* In R. H. Kilmann, I. Kilmann, & Associates. *Making organizations competitive: Enhancing networks and relationships across traditional boundaries.* San Francisco: Jossey-Bass (pp. 156-175).

DeYoung, H. G. (1990, Feb. 19) Tiny resistor maker keeps its eyes on the Baldridge prize. *Electronic Business.*

Drucker, P. F. (1973) *Management: Tasks, responsibilities, practices.* New York: Harper & Row.

Kanter, R. M. (1989) *When giants learn to dance: Mastering the challenges of strategy, management, and careers in the 1990's.* New York: Simon & Schuster.

Kaufman, R. (1989, Feb.) Who is the client? Who benefits? *Performance & Instruction.*

Kaufman, R. (1990, June) Performance technology and quality management: Conflict or new partnership? *Educational Technology.*

Kaufman, R. (1991, Dec.) Toward total quality "plus." *Training, Vol. 28, No. 12.*

Kaufman, R. (1992a) *Strategic planning plus: An organizational guide.* Newbury Park, CA: Sage Publishing.

Kaufman, R. (1992b) *Mapping educational success.* Newbury Park, CA: Corwin Press, Division of Sage.

Kaufman, R., Stith, M., & Kaufman, J. (1992, Feb.) Extending performance technology to improve strategic market planning. *Performance & Instruction.*

Peters, T. (1987) *Thriving on chaos: Handbook for a management revolution.* New York: Alfred A. Knopf.

Forms

Current status of the outputs	Sources

Form 3.1. Complete with current quality of the organization's output as indicated by several sources.

Current status of the output	Desired quality	Need(s)

Form 3.2. Complete when determining needs.

Need(s)	Priority

Form 3.3. Macro-level Need(s) Assessment Summary form.

MICRO-LEVEL NEEDS ASSESSMENT

Chapter 4

Key points:

- What is Micro-level Needs Assessment?

- When and why do a Micro-level Needs Assessment.

- Payoffs and consequences of conducting a Micro-level Needs Assessment linked to Macro- and Megal-levels Needs Assessments.

- The tools, techniques, and steps to use to conduct a Micro-level Needs Assessment.

MICRO-LEVEL NEEDS ASSESSMENT—CHAPTER 4

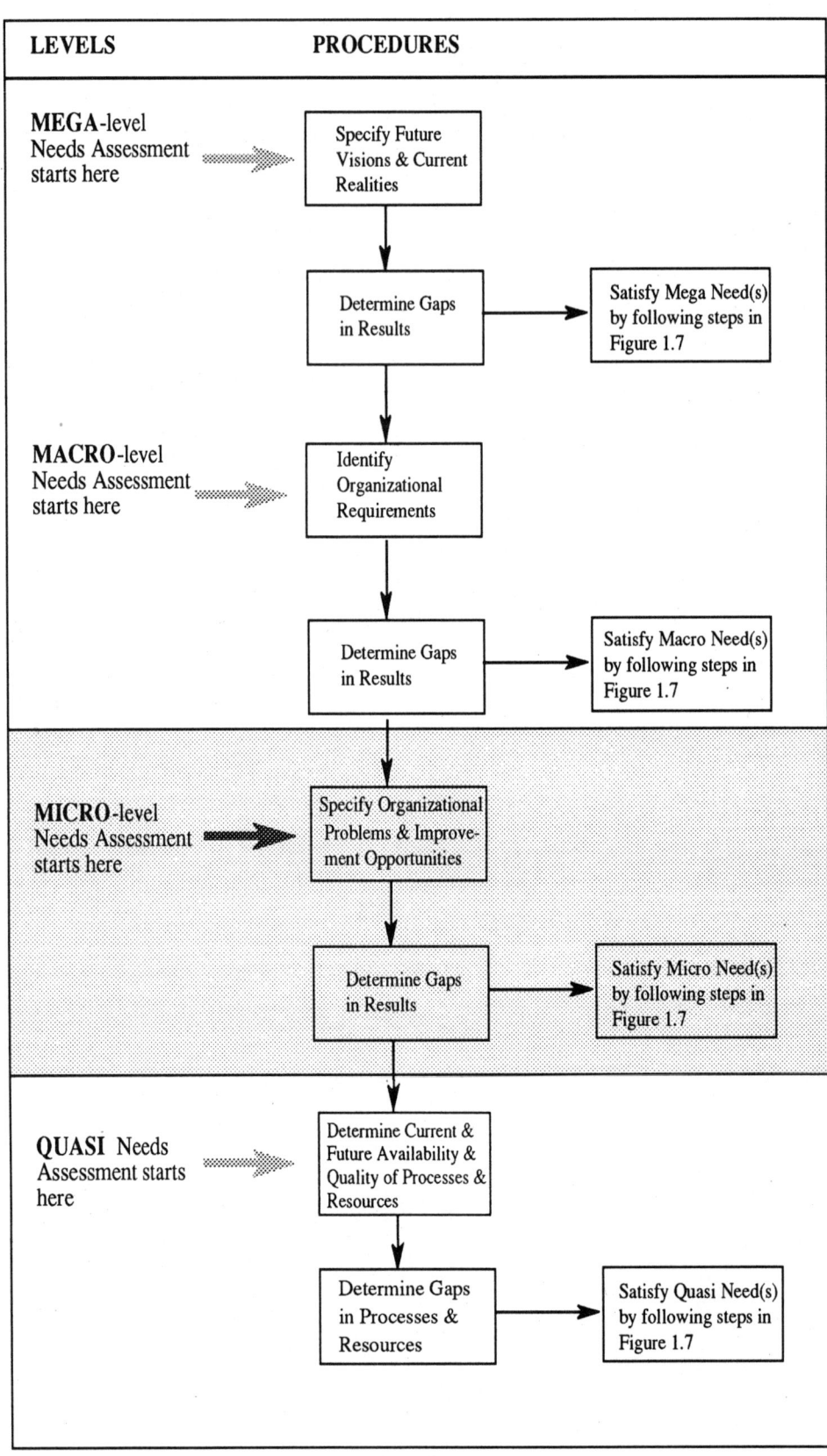

A guide to follow when conducting needs assessment at Mega, Macro, and Micro levels, and when identifying Quasi Needs. The shaded area focuses on information in this chapter.

MICRO-LEVEL NEEDS ASSESSMENT—CHAPTER 4

Consider the following likely scenario: *The Vice-President of Training of the Gold Coin Bank asked for your help in identifying the job-performance requirements of loan officers who specialize in Real-Estate loans. The VP tells you that 80% of the Real-Estate officers have been on the job for less than a year. Additionally, the VP indicates that due to new legislation, changes in the economy, and recent revisions of the Bank's policies, the loan officers' performance specifications (objectives) might require updating. The VP is requesting your help in determining the clarity of performance specifications for Real-Estate Loan Officers. These specifications must include observable and measurable accomplishments.*

What would you do?

This type of a scenario occurs in various organizations more often (sometimes unfortunately so) than the scenarios presented at the beginning of the two previous chapters. The competencies of groups and of individuals are an ongoing concern for supervisors and for managers.

Assuming that:

- the Gold Coin Bank has an organizational mission derived from and contributing to an ideal vision;
- the Bank's deliverables in the Real-Estate area contribute to the accomplishment of the organization's mission.

If you do what you have been asked, your response to the Gold Coin Bank scenario should be to conduct a **Micro-level Needs Assessment.** Note, however, that if either or both of the above two assumptions are incorrect, you should conduct at least a Macro-level Needs Assessment (Chapter 3), and preferably a Mega-level Needs Assessment (Chapter 2).

In this chapter the emphasis is on the correct use of Micro-level Assessment: what it is, why and when it should be used, and what steps to follow to do it correctly and successfully.

What is Micro-level Needs Assessment?

Micro-level Needs Assessment is a process for identifying and resolving gaps between the actual and the desired quality of what is produced by small groups or by individuals within an organization (Kaufman, 1992a).

For example: *Micro-level Needs Assessments may measure the quality of:*

- *Loan portfolios.*
- *Automobile fenders.*
- *Training programs.*
- *Electric-wire connections.*
- *Disk-drives.*

In the case of the Gold Coin Bank, the Vice-President of Training is interested in identifying the job-performance requirements of loan officers. The Gold Coin Bank is focusing on addressing its needs at the **Micro level.**

The process of needs assessment at the Micro level is illustrated in Figure 4.1.

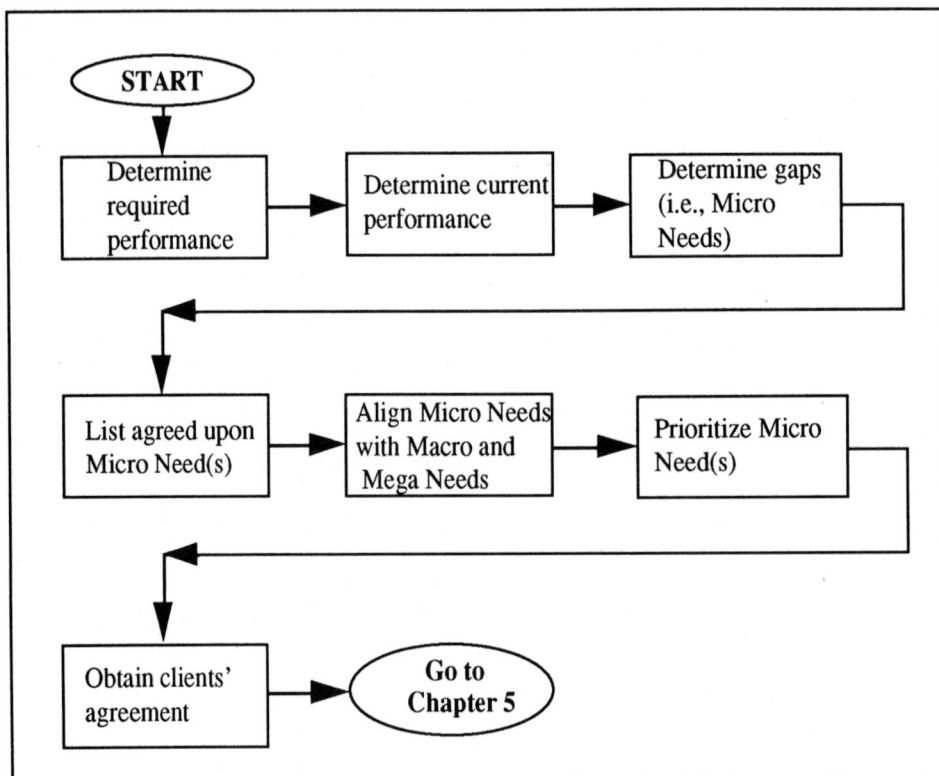

Figure 4.1. Micro needs assessment functions.

When and why should Micro-level Needs Assessment be done?

Whenever an organization decides to purchase new equipment, change its operational procedures, hire new employees, or restructure a task, a Micro-level Needs Assessment may be appropriate.

Essentially, when an organization decides to conduct a Micro-level Needs Assessment, it is concerned with closing the gaps in results related to the quality of what individuals and groups **within** it produce and deliver to others **within** the organization.

For example: *In our scenario, the Gold Coin Bank is interested in a Micro level target–improving the performance of a group of individuals, Real-Estate Loan Officers.*

Note, however, that a Micro-level Needs Assessment is most appropriate when it is aligned and fits with the organization's Mega- and Macro-level Needs Assessments.

The quality of performance of groups and individuals within a company is important primarily in terms of its effect on the quality of the company's deliverables, measured by customer satisfaction (i.e., Macro level—see Chapter 3), and in terms of the ultimate impact, usefulness and appeal to external clients (i.e., Mega level—see Chapter 2).

For example: *A health-care organization, concerned with the performance of its laboratory staff, decided to do a needs assessment to determine the gaps between the current and required quality of blood samples collected from patients. The quality of the laboratory staff's work can be measured by the percentage of inconclusive blood test analyses that are due to inadequate or contaminated blood samples. Consequences of poor-quality blood samples might include having to repeat the collection procedure (thus causing pain, stress, and inconvenience to patients). Furthermore, poor blood samples may cause incorrect patient diagnosis or delay in diagnosis (which could potentially result in incorrect treatment or no treatment and therefore complications and possibly even death).*

The point we are trying to emphasize here is that you should never attempt to do a Micro-level Needs Assessment "in a vacuum." The quality of what individuals and groups within organizations produce and deliver affects the overall output of the organization and will ultimately have impact on the organization's external clients. Starting off by defining what that external impact should be (or at least could be) is the best way to ensure that we can get there.

How to do a Micro-level Needs Assessment

The scope of needs assessment at the Micro level requires that attention be given to the quality of accomplishments of individuals and groups within an organization.

The following are the specific steps and procedures for doing a Micro-level Needs Assessment.

Step 1. Determine individuals' and/or groups' required performance in terms of measurable accomplishments.

A required performance indicates the acceptable type and quality (standard) of accomplishment required of individuals or groups.

For example: *The performance requirements for the Real-Estate Loan Officers at the Gold Coin Bank may include:*

- *At least $25,000,000 of secured commercial Real-Estate loans properly processed per annum.*
- *At least $2,500,000 of secured individual Real-Estate loans (mortgages) properly processed per annum.*
- *No rejections of loans processed by any Real-Estate Loan Officer.*

Required performance should be described in terms of precise, measurable results; i.e., what evidence or data would indicate accomplishment at the acceptable level.

Data (facts and perceptions—*hard* and *soft* data) must be collected to determine the criteria and standards expected of the required performance.

The *hard* data are provided by the performance information. Some indicators may include:

- Acceptable units (quality) at each stage of a production line.
- Acceptable number of completed forms.

- Approved requests.
- Rejection rates of parts (e.g., parts of a car, partially processed documents, part of a service).

Human partners provide the *soft* data (personal perceptions) such as:

- Values.
- Beliefs.
- Opinions.
- Visions.
- Perceived needs.

Some sources for identifying required performance results (*hard* and *soft* data for the Micro level) may include:

- Supervisors' and managers' ratings.
- Feedback on required quality of products and services from internal clients.
- The organization's policies on standards.
- Legislation on competencies and standards.
- Certification guidelines.

Guidelines for determining the desired quality of individual and/or group performance within your organization:

- Determine the appropriate data sources for each required performance specification.
- Obtain the necessary hard and soft data for each required performance specification.
- Present the data you collected on the desired quality of each required performance specification to your group of planning partners (e.g., managers, supervisors, individual performers, other employees, etc.).
- Identify agreements and disagreements among your planning partners regarding the desired quality of each required performance specification.
- Reconcile any disagreements among your planning partners and reach consensus on the desired quality of each required performance specification.
- State the desired quality of each required performance specification.

Step 2. Determine individuals' and/or groups' current performance status vis-a-vis the required standards established in Step 1.

In order to identify any gaps between the required performance and the present level of accomplishments, it is necessary to assess where we are now—current results—in order to determine the current performance status.

This step is crucial to:

- Determine any performance problems and/or opportunities for improvement.
- Make certain that current accomplishments meeting the desired quality criteria and employee's performance standards are maintained and reinforced to ensure that they continue without any changes.

How to determine current status

The current status is determined by collecting data (*hard* and *soft* data) about each current accomplishment.

Some sources of Micro-level data about the current performance status may include, for example:

- Supervisors and management.
- Performers themselves.
- Internal customer feedback on required quality of products and services.
- Individuals reporting to the performers.
- Tests and training program results.
- Published studies and internal organizational reports.
- Notes taken during observation of performance.
- Job-task analysis.

For example: *In order to determine the current status of the Micro-level needs of the Gold Coin Bank, data were gathered about each item. Where Gold Coin Bank is now vis-a-vis the required performance was identified:*

- *$12,000,000 of secured commercial Real-Estate loans properly processed this year.*

- *$1,000,000 of secured individual Real-Estate loans (mortgages) properly processed this year; of that amount, $300,000 are not secured loans.*
- *12% of loans processed by Real-Estate Loan Officers were rejected this year.*

Guidelines for determining the current status of individual and/or group performance within your organization:

- Determine the appropriate data sources for each performance specification.
- Obtain the necessary hard and soft data for each performance specification.
- Present the data you collected on the current status of each performance specification to your group of planning partners (e.g., managers, supervisors, individual performers, other employees, etc.).
- Identify agreements and disagreements among your planning partners regarding the current status of each performance specification.
- Reconcile any disagreements among your planning partners and reach consensus on the current status of each performance specification.
- State the agreed upon current status of each performance specification.

Step 3. List the identified, agreed upon Micro-level need(s) (i.e., gaps in performance of individuals/groups).

As we have stated earlier in this book, need is defined as the gap between the current and the desired results. Therefore, compare the information you obtained in Steps 1 and 2 and identify the difference between the actual performance and the required performance of individuals and/or groups. If the actual (current) performance is different from the required performance, then you have identified a "gap" in performance—NEED at the Micro level. (See Figure 4.2.)

MICRO-LEVEL NEEDS ASSESSMENT—CHAPTER 4

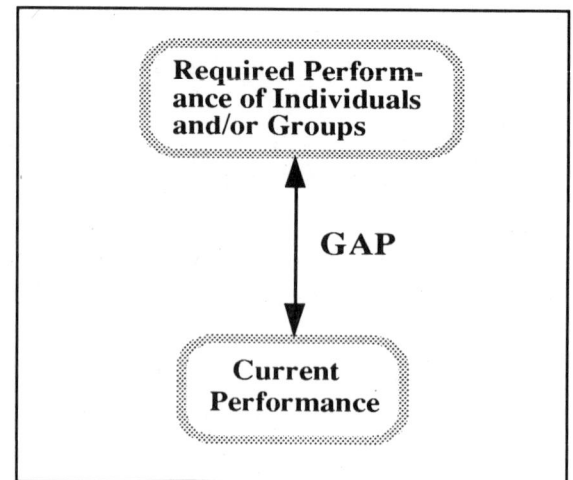

Figure 4.2. Discrepancy between the required performance of individuals and/or groups and its current status.

For example: In our scenario...the following needs were identified:

Required performance	Current performance	Need(s) Gaps in performance
$25,000,000 in commercial loans processed properly per annum.	• $12,000,000 in commercial loans processed properly per annum.	• There is a discrepancy of $13,000,000 in commercial loans processed properly per annum.
$2,500,000 of secured individual Real-Estate loans (mortgages) processed properly per annum.	• $1,000,000 of secured individual Real-Estate loans (mortgages) processed properly this year.	• There is a discrepancy of $1,500,000 of secured individual Real-Estate loans (mortgages) processed properly per annum
No rejections of loans processed by any Real-Estate Loan Officer.	• 12% rejection of loans processed by the Bank's Real-Estate Loan Officers.	• There is a discrepancy of 12% in the rejection rate of processed loans.

Complete Form 4.1 (provided at the end of this chapter) and present it in your meeting with your planning partners. Reach agreement with the planning partners on the identified needs you listed.

Micro-Level Needs Assessment—Chapter 4

Step 4. Align the needs identified at the Micro-level with the vision and mission of your organization.

The main purpose of this step is to compare the needs identified and their alignment with the organization's Macro- and Mega-level needs, vision, and mission.

For example: *In our scenario...The Gold Coin Bank is concerned with the quality of the performance of Real-Estate Loan Officers, as measured by properly processed loans. If loans are processed properly, they can be approved to customers, who then will be satisfied with the service. They will not complain about attitude, accuracy of reporting, and red tape. These customers will continue to use the services of the Gold Coin Bank and recommend the Bank to other potential customers.*

While Micro-level Needs Assessments are more tangible and superficially more practical, they do require large leaps in faith... that fixing small problems will, when taken together, yield organizationally and societally useful results. Rummler and Brache (1990) make a compelling case for not missing what they call "the white spaces of the organization chart." This formulation extends that case to making certain that the "blank spaces" in organizational as well as in external requirements and consequences are also identified and covered. Figure 4.3 shows how needs only identified at the Micro level can miss related needs...missing the blank spaces which come from not aligning the different needs assessment levels by doing a Mega, Macro, and Micro roll-down.

Step 5. Place Micro-level needs in priority order, based on the cost to ignore versus the cost to address each identified need.

Some needs are more critical than others. The most critical needs should be addressed more urgently than others because their consequences will be more severe.

For example: *A gap in the performance of a security guard may cause loss of life or an immediate threat to an individual's life. Such a gap would be more important to resolve than, say, a gap in the performance of the a loan officer.*

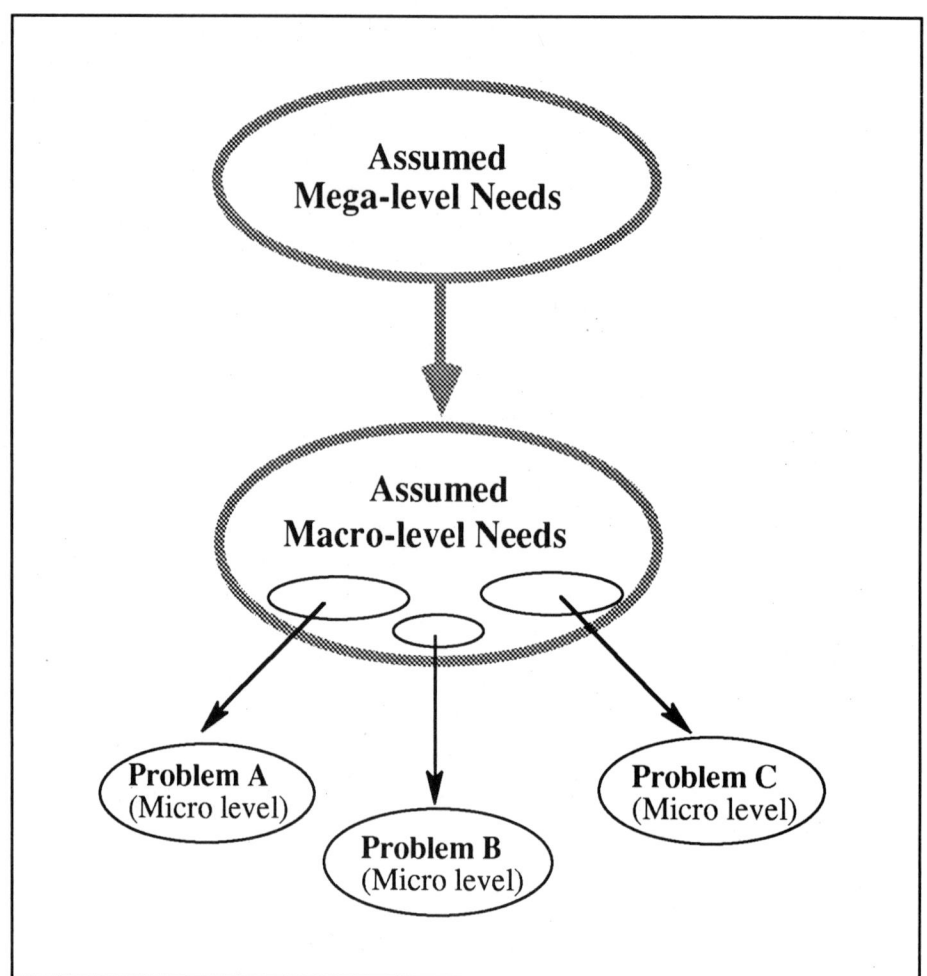

Figure 4.3. Starting needs assessment at Micro level can miss related Macro- and Mega-level needs.

How to prioritize Micro-level needs

Prioritizing Micro-level needs usually requires a judgment call about the relative importance of each need. To do that, we recommend the following:

Guidelines for prioritizing Micro-level needs:

- Determine the criteria to be used for the prioritization. Be sure that the criteria are consistent with your vision and mission. You may take into account the criteria listed and explained in this chapter, and follow the guidelines provided.
- Use the prioritizing method that is most appropriate for your organization. There are several ways to do the ranking. You may use following criteria.

MICRO-LEVEL NEEDS ASSESSMENT—CHAPTER 4

Criteria for prioritizing Micro-level needs

Here are some recommended criteria for prioritizing Micro-level needs:

- Criticality
- Urgency
- Bottom line impact; market trends
- Number of performers
- Time spent to accomplish the required performance

Criticality is a measure of the consequences of inadequate performance. Determining the relative criticality of a need is important because this criterion often overcomes the relative importance of all the other possible prioritizing criteria.

Use the following as benchmarks (or the ones on page 66) for assigning criticality value to identified needs:

Very critical—*Definitely would* contribute to improvement in the quality and/or quantity of products or services provided within the organization.

Moderately critical—*May* contribute to improvement in the quality and/or quantity of products or services provided within the organization.

Not critical—*Probably would not* contribute to improvement in the quality and/or quantity of products or services provided within the organization.

Surplus (candidate for non-funding)—*Will not* contribute to improvement in the quality and/or quantity of products or services provided within the organization.

Urgency. This criterion helps in establishing a schedule for dealing with various identified and anticipated performance problems.

For example: *If a new product is being launched next month, it is urgent to provide basic knowledge and skill about this new product which will contribute to successful delivery and use, before it is launched.*

Bottom Line Impact; Market/Trends. Priority setting is a function of the market requirements and trends, with bottom line impact as the prime determinant.

For example: Competence in sales of commercial Real-Estate loans would have a much higher priority rank in major urban centers than in rural areas with less possible volume in commercial activity.

Number of Performers. The number of performers who have the same need is an important consideration. Needs of a group are usually of greater priority than needs of just one individual, because the consequences of poor performance are magnified by the number of poor performers.

For example: In Unit A, only one loan officer of three is having problems accurately assessing strengths and weaknesses of security. The other two rarely make errors. In Unit B, all three of the loan officers frequently make errors in assessing strengths and weaknesses of security. In Unit B the result is that the number of errors (and therefore the potential losses) is three times greater than in Unit A.

Time Spent Performing. Problems in performance of a task which takes up a large portion of one's time are usually more important to consider than a problem with a task which is rarely performed.

For example: Donna Sun deals with commercial Real-Estate on a daily basis. She works with individual clients on personal Real-Estate loans about once a month (on the average). Knowledge of policies and procedures related to commercial Real-Estate loans is obviously a greater priority to Donna than knowledge of policies and procedures related to personal Real-Estate loans.

Guidelines for prioritizing Micro-level needs:

Consider each of the above criteria in deciding on the relative priority of needs. Do the following:

- Determine the criticality of each need.
- Classify needs into three priority groups:

    1. Very critical.
    2. Moderately critical.
    3. Not critical.

- Using the criteria provided in Form 4.2 (provided at the end of this chater) and any other criteria your planning partners agree on, rank needs within each priority group; the more criteria apply to a specific need, the higher the priority of that need.

For example: *In our scenario...Three of the needs to be resolved at the Gold Coin Bank are: a discrepancy of $13,000,000 in commercial loans; a discrepancy of $1,500,000 in individual mortgages, and a discrepancy of 12% in the rejection rate of all types of Real-Estate loans.*

Gold Coin management decided that the problem with the commercial loans had the greatest bottom-line impact. Furthermore, the market trends seemed to indicate a stronger emphasis on commercial Real-Estate activity. Therefore the discrepancy in commercial loans would be the top priority need to resolve. The 12% in rejected loans would be second in priority, because it was assumed that the majority of the 12% were commercial sector loans. The personal mortgages discrepancy would be last in the priority order because the market trend indicated anticipated decrease in activity in this area.

Step 6. Present your Micro-level needs to your clients for concurrence.

Who are your clients?

Your clients include all your stakeholders, e.g., your company's executive officers, managers, supervisors, individual performers, and groups within the organization who are affected by internally delivered products and services.

Why is client concurrence required?

Client concurrence is important in order to:

- Make certain that no needs have been overlooked.
- Obtain commitment and joint ownership of performers and managers who will help in the implementation of plans to address identified needs.
- Prevent and/or overcome resistance from anyone who might

potentially block the implementation of plans to address identified needs.

How to present Micro-level needs to your clients

Present the Micro-level needs (agreed upon by your planning partners) to your clients by using a needs assessment summary form, such as the one shown in Table 4.1.

A blank Needs Assessment Summary Form is provided at the end of this chapter (see Form 4.3). Use this form to present Micro-level needs to your own clients.

For example: Table 4.1 presents the Micro-level Needs Assessment Summary Form prepared for the Gold Coin Bank.

Needs	Priority
1. A discrepancy of $13,000,000 in commercial loans	Very critical
2. A discrepancy of $1,500,000 in individual mortgages.	Ignore at this time (not critical)
3. A discrepancy of 12% in the rejection rate of all types of Real-Estate loans.	Moderately critical

Table 4.1. Micro-level needs summary table.

Step 7. Identify and list alternative methods and means for addressing your Micro-level need(s), and identify the advantages and disadvantages of each.

There are several possible causes for gaps in individuals' and/or groups' performance (i.e., Micro-level needs). Each requires a different solution (i.e., methods and/or means). Table 4.2 identifies a variety of solutions to performance problems, each solution clearly based on eliminating the cause of the problem. Note that often more than one cause may affect performance and therefore more than one solution (at least one for each cause) would be appropriate.

Table 4.2. Some examples of relating causes and solutions for Micro-level Performance Problems.

IF the cause of a performance problem is that:	THEN the solution may be to:
The performer is not aware of the need, i.e., does not know what the required standard is, by when it must be achieved, how, when reports are due, etc.	• Provide clear guidance and constructive feedback. • Clearly communicate the required performance standards.
The performer is not recognized or rewarded for performance at the required level.	• Ensure that the desired performance is recognized and rewarded.
The environment presents obstacles which make it difficult to perform the task (e.g., inadequate materials, lack of resources, conflicting work responsibilities).	• Provide the necessary resources/equipment/materials. • Remove or minimize obstacles.
The performer exhibits a negative attitude toward the required performance (e.g., refuses to complete an assignment).	• Find out why. • Change the conditions, factors, or activities that contribute to reinforce such attitudes
The performer lacks the skills or knowledge to perform the task as required.	• Provide training. • Provide on-the-job coaching. • Develop job aids.

How to identify methods and means

The basic tool for identifying alternative methods and means as well as determining relative advantages and disadvantages of each is by a methods-means analysis. Chapter 5 provides an outline of the steps and procedures to take when you are identifying the various methods and means you may use to meet your needs.

Chapter Summary

In this chapter we defined Micro-level Needs Assessment and explained when and how to do it.

A Micro-level Needs Assessment is most useful when it is aligned with larger scope Macro- and Mega-level assessments. In doing a Micro-level Needs Assessment you are focusing on the job-performance requirements of individuals, groups, or departments within your organization.

This chapter provides guidance on how to conduct a Micro-level Needs Assessment, with examples of formats and procedures for accomplishing each step in the process.

The key points of this chapter are:

- Micro-level Needs Assessment is the process of identifying the gaps between the actual and the desired accomplishments of an individual or a group, as measured by the quality and quantity of what that individual or group accomplishes within an organization.

- Micro-level Needs Assessment should be conducted to identify, analyze, and evaluate alternative ways and means to resolve any gaps in individual or group performance that may affect an organization's accomplishment of its Macro- and Mega-level objectives.

- The seven major steps for conducting a Micro-level Needs Assessment include:

    1. Determine individuals' and/or groups' required performance in terms of measurable accomplishments.
    2. Determine individuals' and/or groups' current performance status vis-a-vis the required standards established in Step 1.
    3. List the identified, agreed upon Micro-level need(s).
    4. Align the needs identified at the Micro level with the vision and mission of your organization.
    5. Place Micro-level needs in priority order, based on the cost to ignore versus the cost to address each identified need.
    6. Present your Micro-level needs to your clients for concurrence.
    7. Identify and list alternative methods and means for addressing your Micro-level need(s), and identify the advantages and disadvantages of each.

References and Suggested Readings

Carlisle, K. E. (1986) *Analyzing jobs and tasks*. Englewood Cliffs, NJ: Educational Technology Publications.

Harless, J. H. (1975) *An ounce of analysis (is worth a pound of cure)*. Newnan, GA: Harless Performance Guild.

Kaufman, R. (1991, Dec.) Toward total quality "plus." *Training, Vol 28, No. 12*.

Kaufman, R. (1992a) *Strategic planning plus: An organizational guide*. Newbury Park, CA: Sage Publishing.

Kaufman, R. (1992b) *Mapping educational success*. Newbury Park, CA: Corwin Press, Division of Sage.

Kaufman, R. & Herman, J. (1991) *Strategic planning in education: Rethinking, restructuring, revitalizing*. Lancaster, PA: Technomic Publishers.

Mayer, H. & Coldeway, D. O. (1990) *TIP—research report #1: Training and performance improvement needs in business and industry*. Athabasca, Alberta: Athabasca University.

Rummler, G. A. & Brache, E. P. (1990) *Improving performance: How to manage the white space on the organization chart*. San Francisco, CA: Jossey-Bass.

Forms

Required performance	Current performance	Need(s)

Form 4.1. Complete when determining needs.

Prioritize your needs—Check all criteria that apply

Title or description of need:
_____
_____
_____

_____ This need is very critical.
_____ This need is moderately critical.
_____ This need is *not* critical (therefore, ignore it).
_____ This is not a need.

_____ Urgent to address because _____.
_____ High market priority.
_____ More than one performer's need. (How many?_____).
_____ Substantial time is spent accomplishing the required performance.

Form 4.2. Criteria for placing Micro-level needs in priority order.

Micro Need(s)	Priority

Form 4.3. Micro-level Needs Assessment Summary form.

QUASI NEEDS ASSESSMENT

Chapter 5

Key points:

- What is Quasi Needs Assessment?

- When and why do a Quasi Needs Assessment.

- Payoffs and consequences of conducting a Quasi Needs Assessment linked to Mega-, Macro-, and Micro-level Needs Assessments.

- The tools, techniques, and steps to use to conduct a Quasi Needs Assessment.

- Why Quasi Needs Assessment is sometimes called "training needs assessment"—an inaccurate label for an important tool.

Quasi Needs Assessment—Chapter 5

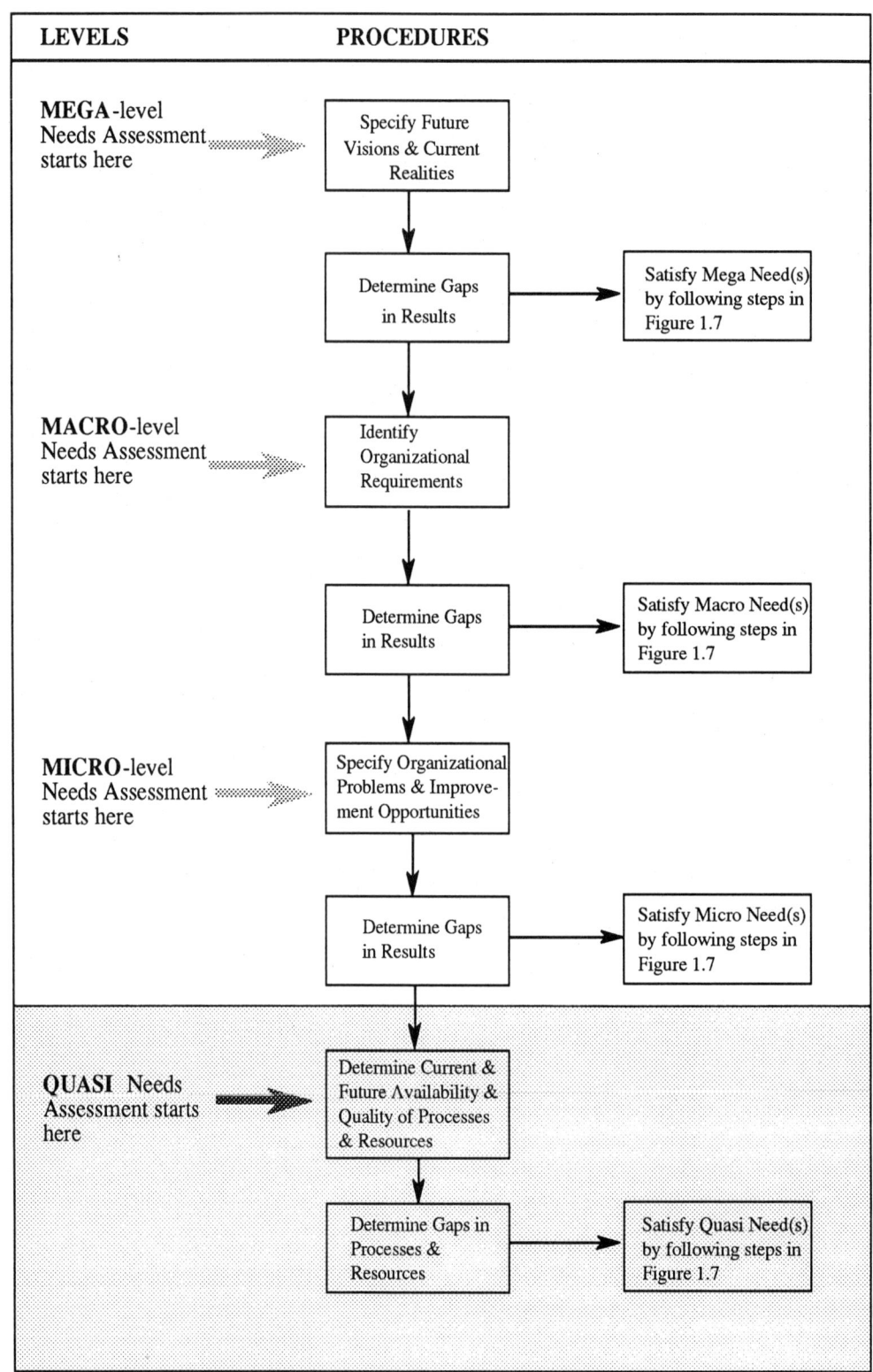

A guide to follow when conducting needs assessment at Mega, Macro, and Micro levels, and when identifying quasi needs. The shaded area focuses on information in this chapter.

QUASI NEEDS ASSESSMENT—CHAPTER 5

Consider the following likely scenario: *The weekly meeting is in progress. Once again the Sales Managers of the Fitrend Company's three district offices complain that their new salespeople are away too long from their regular duties when they participate in the Sales Training program. At this point, the managers agree on the quality of the skills acquired by their salespeople. They are asking you, in the Training Department, to maintain the quality of the training and the types of skills learned by the salespeople. The managers' concerns are the length of time spent at the Training Center, the cost of the training, and the lack of use of modern technologies. Therefore, the managers ask if it is possible to train the salesforce more efficiently. And even though they have to reduce their budget allocation for training, they would still like to receive the current quality and effectiveness in all training programs; but they would also like the training to be more efficient and less costly. You have to present a proposal to the managers dealing with these issues by next week.*

What would you do?

This scenario occurs in many companies. When money is tight—and usually it seems to be tight (in good times and bad)—"doing more with less" is usually the requirement. For example, it is common to reduce funds for training when cutting company budgets. In addition, it is assumed that if employees spend less time in training sessions, they may be more "productive" selling or producing the company's goods and services.

In this case, managers are concerned with the efficiency of training: better use of their resources and methods to produce the results desired. Because we know where we are going (or believe we do), we may conduct a **Quasi Needs Assessment.** This chapter presents information on what a Quasi Needs Assessment is all about and how to do it successfully.

What is Quasi Needs Assessment?

Quasi Needs Assessment is the process for identifying gaps in methods-means, procedures, and how-to-do-its in order to efficiently meet performance requirements (or objectives). Quasi Needs Assessment also identifies gaps in availability and/or quality of the human, capital, and material resources used. This process is also known as a methods-means analysis (Kaufman, 1992a, b).

Note that gaps between current and desired processes and resources are termed "Quasi needs" (Kaufman, 1988) to highlight that they are not gaps in results but rather gaps in processes and/or inputs. Quasi Needs Assessment is also termed methods-means analysis because through the analysis, possible tactics and tools are identified for achieving organizational results, and the advantages and disadvantages of each are revealed and noted. The process requires you to ask and answer:

- What are the gaps in methods and means?
- What are the gaps in resources?
- What methods-means are available?
- What are the relative advantages of each?

Examples of Quasi needs are:

- Increase the number of loan applications.
- Prepare a new fiscal budget that is "tighter" than last year's.
- Train the multicultural workforce.
- Conduct a needs assessment.

When and why should a Quasi Needs Assessment be done?

Needs assessment assures that opportunities, purposes, and related solutions will be practical and results-oriented, not just process-oriented. Needs assessment can help you in identifying and *selecting the right job* before *doing the job right*.

Quasi Needs Assessment assures that the procedures and resources (methods and means) you use will help you in *doing the job right*—and most effectively and efficiently.

A needs assessment provides the needs—gaps in results. It then allows you to analyze the causes of these gaps in order to determine what it will take to improve results. Determining of the origins and causes of needs is called *needs analysis* (Kaufman & Valentine, 1989). From the data generated by a needs assessment and then a needs analysis (the order is very important), you may identify ways and means to close the gaps—these ways and means are **Quasi needs.**

The process of identifying and selecting the best ways and means to address needs has several labels: methods-mean analysis, Quasi Needs Assessment, training requirements analysis, and *training needs assessment*. *Training needs assessment* is an unfortunate label, for it tends to encourage some people—in spite of caveats by some authors (e.g., Rossett, 1987)—to start their needs assessment and planning with a solution—training—before identifying the gaps in results and before selecting training as the solution. Still, the generic tools of *training needs assessment* are useful when you *do* know that training (or some other intervention) will be required.

Sometimes the answer to improving results does lie in training, but often it lies elsewhere (cf. Rummler & Brache, 1990). Before you pick a solution, or intervention (any how-to-get-the-job-done methodology), make sure you collect needs assessment data that will help you find the important gaps between current results and desired ones. Then, knowing the gaps in results (and payoffs), you can sensibly pick the best way to get from where you are to where you want to be.

The relationships between the gaps in organizational efforts (i.e., Quasi Needs Assessment) and organizational results (i.e., Micro- and Macro-level Needs Assessments) along with societal impact (i.e., Mega-level Needs Assessment) are presented in Figure 5.1.

Thus, when you are interested in finding out the most efficient tools, techniques, interventions, and resources you may do a Quasi Needs Assessment.

For example: *In our scenario...Managers are asking for a more efficient and less costly way to accomplish the same results (or even better ones) as now delivered.*

In order to determine what are the best methods and means to produce the same results, a Quasi Needs Assessment or methods-means analysis can be conducted.

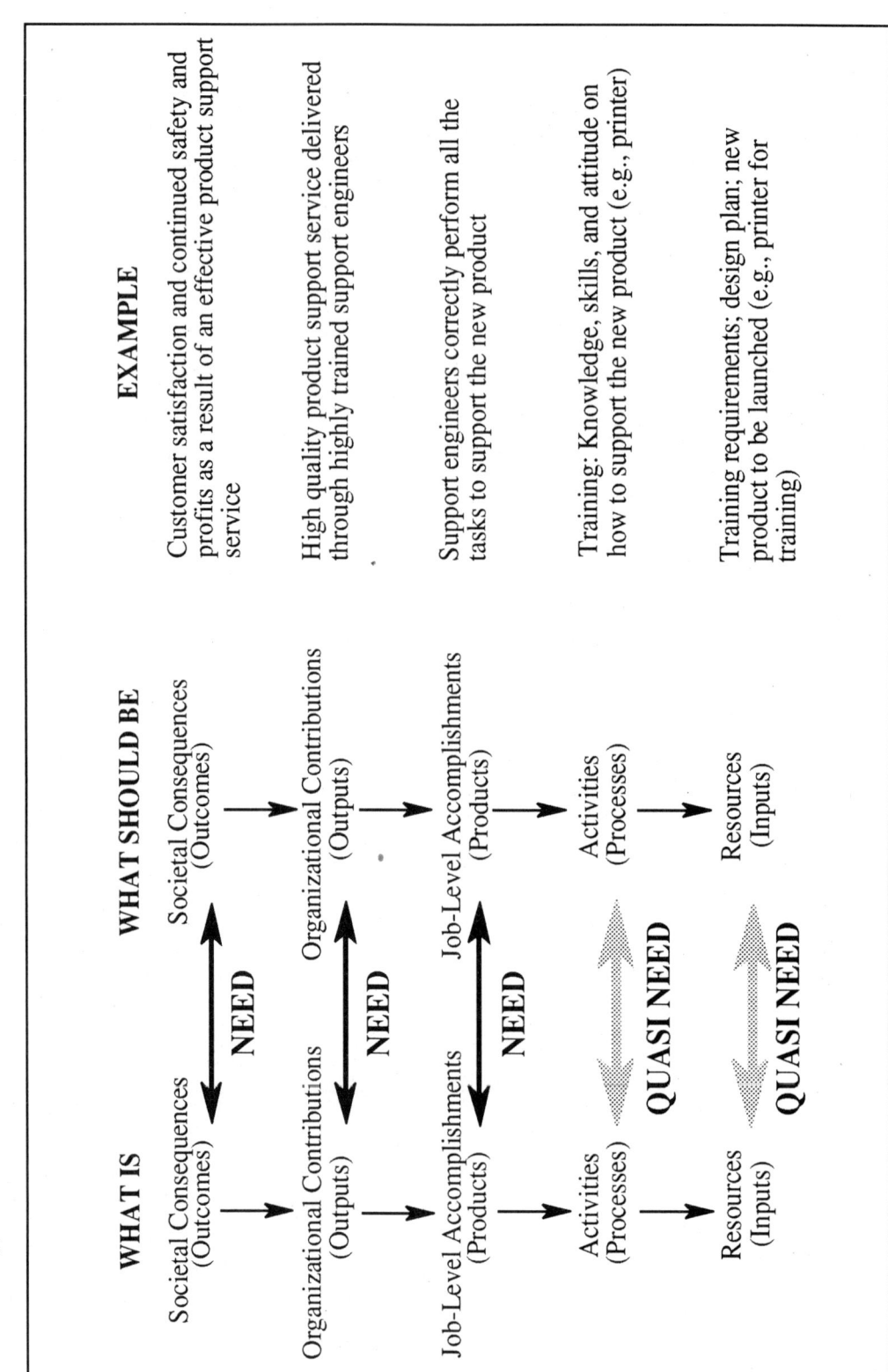

Figure 5.1. Relationships among the different levels of Needs Assessment. The first 3 levels (dark arrows) deal with Needs, the last two (shaded arrows) are Quasi Needs.

The Quasi Needs Assessment and/or method-means analysis provides information about tactics and tools (ways and means) required to meet specified performance requirements. It begins as soon as performance requirements have been identified.

How to do a Quasi Needs Assessment

Note that we have defined **Quasi Needs Assessment** as the same as **methods-means analysis**, which identifies what how-to-do-its are available for delivering the required organizational and societal results and payoffs. The steps to accomplish the analysis (or the Quasi Needs Assessment) may start at different points depending on whether or not you have done a needs assessment. Table 5.1 specifies the steps to follow when conducting a Quasi Needs Assessment, depending on your starting point.

Therefore, decide where you are starting the Quasi Needs Assessment and follow these steps.

Step 1. Specify the desired availability and/or quality of the organizational resources and methods.

In order to determine if there is any gap, it is useful to determine what the quality of the resources or methods should be to achieve desired objectives.

For example: *In our Fitrend scenario...the desired availability and/or quality of methods and resources could be:*

- *Managers expect a training program that will allow the salespeople to dedicate at least 75% of the working week to their regular sales duties.*
- *The salespeople should acquire the necessary skills without leaving the office more than 1/2 day per week, if at all.*
- *Each salesperson should receive a set of validated job aids with selling guidelines to use on the job.*
- *Managers also request, as an ideal situation, the availability of a senior sales trainer 24 hours a day, perhaps as a "hotline" available to the salesperson anywhere in the world.*

If you are starting a Quasi Needs Assessment, do the following:	If you have already done a Needs Assessment at Mega, Macro, and/or Micro levels, do the following:
Step 1. Specify the desired availability and/or quality of the organizational resources and methods.	Step 1. Identify alternative ways and means for addressing the identified Quasi Need(s) and Need(s).
Step 2. Determine the current quality and/or availability of the organizational efforts (i.e., resources and methods).	Step 2. Identify advantages of each possible method and means available to get the job done.
Step 3. Determine Quasi Needs—the gaps between the desired and the current status of the organizational efforts (i.e., inputs and processes).	Step 3. Identify constraints and eliminate them if possible.
Step 4. Align the Quasi Need(s) identified with the needs at Mega, Macro, and Micro levels.	Step 4. Present alternative methods-means for addressing all agreed upon Needs and Quasi Needs to your clients, for agreement on the methods and means to be selected for action.
Step 5. Place Quasi Need(s) in order of importance, based on the cost to ignore versus the cost to address each identified Quasi Need(s).	Step 5. Plan, implement, evaluate, and revise as required.
Step 6. Identify alternative ways and means to close the identified Quasi Need(s) and to Need(s).	
Step 7. Identify advantages of each possible method and means available to get the job done.	
Step 8. Identify constraints and eliminate them if possible.	
Step 9. Present alternative methods-means for addressing all agreed upon Needs and Quasi Needs to your clients, for agreement on the methods and means to be selected for action.	
Step 10. Plan, implement, evaluate, and revise as required.	

Table 5.1. Steps to follow based on the starting point of the Needs Assessment.

How to determine the desired availability and/or quality of the organization's efforts (resources and methods)

The organization may define the desired quality and/or availability of its efforts to achieve objectives by collecting related data.

Data (facts and figures—*hard* and *soft* data) must be collected to determine the criteria and standards expected of the resources and methods to be used.

Sources for Quasi needs data may include:

- Users of the resources/methods.
- Research on methods, media, instructional technology.
- Legislation on standards, where applicable.
- Subject-matter experts.
- Supervisory mandates.
- Strategic plans of the company.
- Needs assessment data from Mega, Macro, and Micro levels.

Guidelines for determining the desired availability and/or quality of organizational efforts:

- Determine the appropriate data sources for identifying the desired availability and/or quality of organizational efforts.
- Obtain the necessary hard and soft data.
- Present the data you collected to your group of planning partners (e.g., managers, supervisors, individual performers, other employees, etc.).
- Identify agreements and disagreements among your planning partners regarding the desired availability and/or quality of organizational efforts.
- Reconcile any disagreements among your planning partners and reach consensus on the desired availability and/or quality of organizational efforts.
- State the desired availability and/or quality of organizational efforts by recording your findings.

Step 2. Determine the current availability and/or quality of the organization's efforts.

The current status regarding the quality and availability of various resources and methods (i.e., organizational efforts) is important to identify, in order to determine if there is any Quasi need to resolve. Nevertheless, if there is no gap between the desired and the current levels of the organization's efforts, it is still very important to maintain (and *not* change) the resources and methods that are effective and efficient in accomplishing the organization's desired Micro-, Macro-, and Mega-level results.

How to determine the current status of the organization's efforts

Data (facts and perceptions, *hard* and *soft* data) must be collected to determine the current status of the inputs and processes required to accomplish organizational results.

The *hard data (independently verifiable facts and figures)* are provided by performance information. Some of these indicators may include:

- Objectives accomplished.
- Number of training hours offered.
- Production indicators (e.g., rejects, time for production, etc.).
- List of manufacturing methods used.

The human partners provide the *soft data (personal perceptions)* such as:

- Values.
- Beliefs.
- Opinions.
- Visions.
- Perceived needs.

Some sources for deriving Quasi needs (*hard* and *soft*) data may include:

- Cost analysis reports.
- Evaluation reports/Users' feedback.
- Managers' complaints/Feedback.
- Report on needs assessment at the Mega, Macro, and Micro levels.
- Union reports.

- Sales documents.
- Quality Control/Assurance data.
- Total Quality Management data.

For example: *Continuing with our scenario... according to sales trainees' feedback, the current training program does not allow them to promptly serve the clients, and therefore, the productivity of their sales has decreased by 15% during the duration of the training program (as documented in the Treasurer's Report on this year's first quarter sales). There is also a reduction in the company outputs delivered to customers, as indicated in the company's latest annual report. Managers and trainees also indicated the lack of assistance after the training is over—they complained about the lack of job-related training materials which could be used on the job (rather than in training sessions); they also complained about the lack of updated sales tips, new product descriptions, and policy specifications (updates).*

Guidelines for determining the current availability and/or quality of organizational efforts:

- Determine the appropriate data sources for identifying the current availability and/or quality of organizational efforts.
- Obtain the necessary hard and soft data.
- Present the data you collected to your group of planning partners (e.g., managers, supervisors, individual performers, other employees, etc.).
- Identify agreements and disagreements among your planning partners regarding the current availability and/or quality of organizational efforts.
- Reconcile any disagreements among your planning partners and reach consensus on the current availability and/or quality of organizational efforts.
- State the current availability and/or quality of organizational efforts by recording your findings.

Step 3. Determine Quasi needs—the gaps between the desired and the current status of the organizational efforts.

Any discrepancy between the desired and the current status of the organizational efforts (methods and means/processes and inputs), is a Quasi need. (See Figure 5.2.)

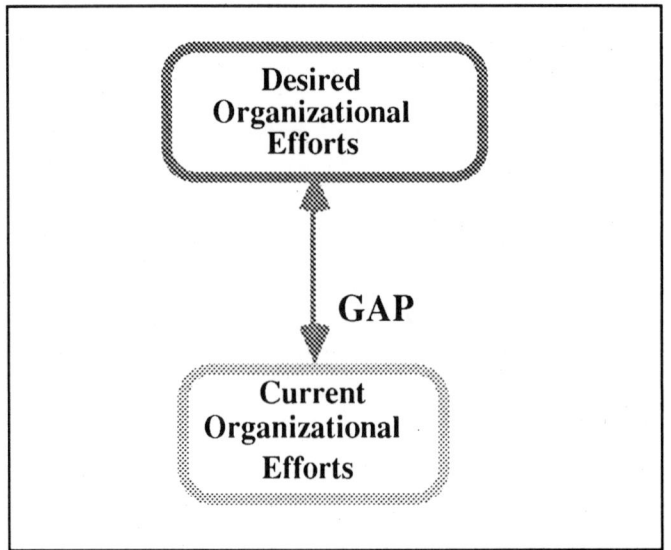

Figure 5.2. Discrepancy between the desired organizational efforts and their current status.

For example: In our scenario...the manager and training department representatives may complete a table such as the one below. Note that the information included in this example Quasi Needs Assessment table (Table 5.2) was derived **after** a Needs Assessment had been done at the Macro and Micro levels:

Current status of the organizational efforts	Desired status	Quasi Needs Gaps in methods-means
Training at the Training Center	Available on job location to increase sales	Appropriate and convenient location
Training length interferes with regular duties	No more than 25% of the regular duties time	Adapt training time to regular duties requirements
Lack of job-related training materials to use on the job	Availability of training materials in the job	Availability of validated training materials on the job
No post-training assistance	24-hour assistance	Provide 24-hour assistance/ access to advice

Table 5.2. A hypothetical Quasi Needs Assessment table for Fitrend.

Guidelines for determining Quasi needs:

Complete Form 5.1 (provided at the end of this chapter) and present it in your meeting with your planning partners. Reach an agreement with the planning partners on the identified Quasi needs you listed.

Step 4. Align the Quasi needs identified with the needs at Micro, Macro, and Mega levels.

The main purpose of this step is to compare the Quasi needs identified and determine if there is a linkage with the needs identified at the other three needs assessment levels: Micro, Macro, and Mega.

For example: *In our scenario...the training department should determine if the linkage among the three levels is maintained. For instance:*

- *The training methodology (processes, means) and resources required lead to improving the quality of skills to be mastered (Micro level) as a result of the training program.*
- *Lack of time dedicated to sales during the training period. This situation may influence a decrease in the organizational outputs delivered to customers (Macro level).*
- *Effective product support service. This situation influences the customer' satisfaction and continued safety and profits (Mega level).*

Step 5. Place Quasi need(s) in order of importance, based on the cost to ignore versus the cost to address each.

Some Quasi needs are more critical than others and should be addressed more urgently.

Hence, Quasi needs, just like needs, must be placed in priority order. This requires an indicator, usually an estimate of the criticality of each gap based on the cost to ignore versus the cost to address the identified need(s). Furthermore, consider the contribution of each method-means to addressing the Micro-, Macro-, and Mega-level needs previously identified.

How to prioritize Quasi needs

Prioritizing Quasi needs usually requires a judgment about the relative contribution of each Quasi need to the meeting or reducing of needs at the

Micro, Macro, and Mega levels. To do that, we recommend that you follow the guidelines provided here:

Guidelines for prioritizing Quasi Needs:

- Answer the following questions:
  - What will it *cost to address* the **Quasi Need**?
  - What will it *cost to ignore* the **Quasi Need**?

Note: "Cost" as used here relates not only to immediate dollar outlay but also to costs in terms of future money outlays, resources, and other factors such as image, social good, opportunity lost, marketability, and future organizational survival and contributions.

- Determine the criteria to be used for the prioritization. Be sure that the criteria are consistent with your organizational mission. What your client wants (e.g., 24-hour assistance) won't be useful unless the assistance has the information required for successful job performance. This is a good example of how means must contribute to ends.

- Use the prioritizing method that is most appropriate for your organization. There are several ways to prioritize Quasi needs. One is to sort the identified Quasi needs into categories that fit your situation. For instance, the categories might be:

  Very critical—*Definitely would* contribute to effectively and efficiently addressing Micro-, Macro-, and Mega-level needs.
  Moderately critical—*May* contribute to effectively and efficiently addressing Micro-, Macro-, and Mega-level needs.
  Not critical—*Probably would not* contribute to effectively and efficiently addressing Micro-, Macro-, and Mega-level needs.
  Surplus (candidate for non-funding)—*Will not* contribute to effectively and efficiently addressing Micro-, Macro-, and Mega-level needs.

For example: Using the Fitrend Company scenario—here is a Table (Table 5.3) indicating the prioritization of the Quasi needs identified and a justification of the priority order given by the partners:

Table 5.3. Prioritization of Quasi Needs.

Quasi Needs–Gaps in methods-means	Type of priority	Why/Rationale
To offer the training in a way that takes only 25% of the time dedicated to regular duties.	Very Critical	- Sales and profits cannot decrease - Internal customers should be satisfied
To identify an appropriate location to offer the training mainly "on location" (i.e., on-the-job).	Very Critical	Same as above
To provide training materials for on-the-job use.	Very Critical	Same as above
To provide 24-hour assistance.	Moderately Critical	Same as above, and by satisfying previous Quasi needs, this one is expected to be eliminated or turned over to operations for possible on-line specifications up-date.

A blank form for prioritizing needs is provided at the end of this chapter (see Form 5.2). Use this form to present a prioritized list of Quasi needs to your own clients/planning partners.

Step 6. **(or Step 1 if you have already identified needs at the Mega, Macro, and/or Micro levels). Identify alternative methods and means for addressing the identified Quasi need(s) and for need(s).**

Methods are procedures and techniques we use to meet or reduce needs. Examples of methods may include:

Training	Tactical planning
Team building	Economic analysis
Managing by objectives	Operating
Strategic planning	Recruiting
Total Quality Management	Needs Assessment
Mentoring	Quasi Needs Assessment

Means are tools and resources we use to address needs. Examples of means may include:

Books	Objectives
Forklift trucks	Company vision
Computers	Personnel
Surgical tools	Budget

Why identify alternative methods and means?

We identify alternative methods-means in order to identify the various possible resources, tools, and ways by which our objectives and missions can be accomplished. This will force the consideration of alternative ways to address needs. It will encourage us not to automatically attempt to do things—employ methods and means—the way they have been done in the past. It provides the opportunity to be creative, to develop new ways to meet needs.

Guidelines for identifying alternative methods and means:

- Identify data sources. You may consult technical journals, research data bases, experts, consultants, university centers, professional organizations, etc.
- Collect all the data possible without limiting yourself to what you are familiar with.
- Explore new ideas, brainstorm, create, innovate.
- List at least two possible methods-means for each performance requirement.
- Complete a table (such as Table 5.4) for each of the needs and Quasi needs identified.

Step 7. (or Step 2 if you have already identified needs at the Mega, Macro, and/or Micro levels.) **Identify advantages and disadvantages of each possible method and means available to get the job done.**

After a similar table is completed, the advantages and disadvantages can be listed for further analysis. In this way a feasibility study is being conducted. A typical table is Table 5.5. A blank table (such as the one in Table 5.5) is provided for you to use with your own clients/planning partners at the end of this chapter (Form 5.3).

Performance requirement(s)	Possible methods and means
1. Printer will cost 2% less than in first quarter without diminishing its quality.	1. Reduce manufacturing costs by using robotics. 2. Change some parts for less expensive price and same quality. 3. Reduce profits desired.
2. Technical assistance will be provided during 24-hours, in the two main languages of the workforce (i.e., English and Chinese).	1. Use a type of "hot-line" with three shifts of bilingual operators. 2. On-line assistance. 3. Use of hypertext to produce "questions and answers" available in the mainframe for use as required.

Table 5.4. Table to determine possible methods and means.

Performance Requirements	Possible Methods-Means	Advantages	Disadvantages
Technical assistance will be provided during 24-hours, in the two main languages (i.e., English and Chinese).	1. Use a type of "hot-line" with hree shifts of bilingual operators. 2. On-line assistance. 3. Use of hypertext to produce "questions and answers" available in the mainframe for use as required.	- Prompt response to inquiries. - Available 24-hours. - Prompt response to inquiries. - May include answers unknown to operators.	- Difficult to hire bilingual operators with desired technical skills. - Lack of computer skills of most salespeople. - Same as both items above. - Expensive to create and upadate.

Table 5.5. Table to specify advantages and disadvantages of methods-means previously identified.

Step 8. (or Step 3 if you have already identified needs at the Mega, Macro, and/ or Micro levels.) Identify constraints and eliminate them if possible.

What is a constraint?

A constraint is a condition that makes it impossible to meet a performance requirement (Kaufman, 1988).

Guidelines for eliminating constraints:

Identify all the constraints and make a list, then consider this option:

- Change the performance requirement(s).

For example: *In our scenario...the performance requirement specifies that technical assistance should be provided 24-hours a day. The main constraint to do so is the availability of personnel due to budget limitations which cannot be eliminated at this time. Hence, the performance requirement is modified accordingly. The technical assistance will be provided during daytime only until the new fiscal year.*

- Verify if the change is still responsive to the documented needs and/or Quasi needs. If it is, do the next step, and be careful that the new performance requirement is responsive to the identified need(s).
- Create, invent a new or different way to meet the requirement(s)—a methods-means which previously did not exist.
- If none of the above work, then stop since you cannot get where you want to go from here.

The above described guidelines are represented in an algorithm in Figure 5.3.

Step 9. Present alternative methods and means for addressing all agreed upon needs and Quasi needs to your clients for agreement on the methods and means to be selected for action.

If you have followed the steps for conducting a Quasi Needs Assessment, you have a list of the possible methods and means (solutions) for meeting performance requirements, including advantages and disadvantages of each.

The next steps will be to:

- Select the solution.
- Plan its implementation.

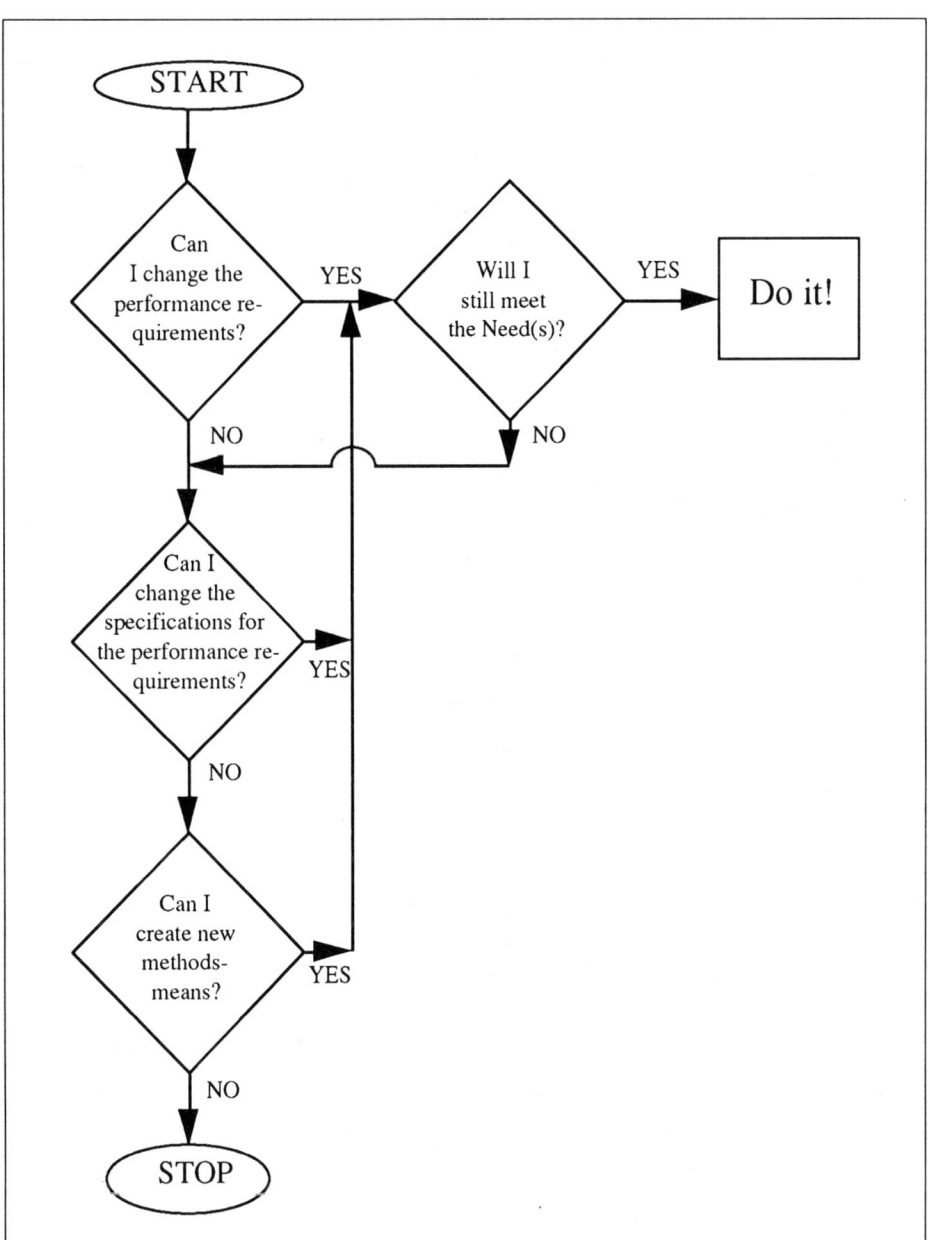

Figure 5.3. Algorithm on how to eliminate constraints (Kaufman, 1992a).

- Implement solution.
- Evaluate to determine effectiveness and efficiency.
- Revise as required...to produce the desired results.

These steps are discussed in the next chapter.

Chapter Summary

A Quasi Needs Assessment is a process for identifying and resolving gaps between the actual and the desired quality and/or availability of organizational efforts—inputs and processes.

Quasi Needs Assessment is also termed methods-means analysis (and sometimes *training needs assessment*) because through the analysis, possible tactics and tools are identified for achieving organizational results.

The process used to conduct a Quasi Needs Assessment is similar to the process used for other levels of needs assessment. They both address gaps. A Quasi Needs Assessment is different, in that it:

- Uses or assumes that needs have been assessed and are being used.
- Identifies gaps in resources and/or methods and means.
- Places the gaps in means in priority order.

Remember that when an organization decides to conduct a Quasi Needs Assessment, it is concerned with closing the gaps in organizational efforts. These are most effective if they are related to gaps in results at the Mega, Macro, and Micro levels.

In this chapter, we defined Quasi Needs Assessment and explained when, why, and how to do one.

The steps to use when conducting a Quasi Needs Assessment are:

1. Specify the desired availability and/or quality of the organization's resources and methods.
2. Determine the current quality and/or availability of the organization's efforts.
3. Determine Quasi needs—the gaps between the desired and the current organizational efforts.
4. Align the Quasi needs identified with the needs at Mega, Macro, and Micro levels.
5. Place Quasi needs in order of importance, based on the cost to ignore versus the cost to address each identified Quasi need.

6. (or Step 1 if you have already identified needs at Mega, Macro, and/or Micro levels.) Identify alternative methods and means for addressing the identified Quasi need(s) and/or need(s).
7. (or Step 2 if you have already identified needs at the Mega, Macro, and/or Micro levels.) Identify advantages and disadvantages of each possible method and means available to get the job done.
8. (or Step 3 if you have already identified needs at the Mega, Macro, and/or Micro levels.) Identify constraints and eliminate them if possible.
9. Present alternative methods and means for addressing all agreed upon needs and Quasi needs to your clients, for agreement on the methods and means to be selected for action.

References and Suggested Readings

Kaufman, R. (1988) *Planning educational systems: A results-based approach.* Lancaster, PA: Technomic Publishing.

Kaufman, R. (1992a) *Strategic planning plus: An organizational guide.* Newbury Park, CA: Sage Publishing.

Kaufman, R. (1992b) *Mapping educational success.* Newbury Park, CA: Corwin Press, Division of Sage.

Kaufman, R. & Valentine, G. (1989, Nov.) Relating needs assessment and needs analysis. *Performance & Instruction.*

Rossett, A. (1987) *Training needs assessment.* Englewood Cliffs, NJ: Educational Technology Publications.

Rummler, G. A. & Brache, A. P. (1990) *Improving performance: How to manage the white space on the organization chart.* San Francisco: Jossey-Bass.

Forms

Current status of the organizational efforts	Desired status	Quasi Needs (Gaps in methods-means)

Form 5.1. Determining Quasi needs.

Quasi-Needs-Gaps in methods-means	Type of priority	Why/Rationale

Form 5.2. Prioritization of needs.

Performance Requirements	Possible Methods-means	Advantages	Disadvantages

Form 5.3. Form to specify advantages and disadvantages of methods-means.

NEEDS ASSESSMENT & ORGANIZATIONAL EFFECTIVENESS

Chapter 6

Key points:

- Relating needs assessment to strategic planning and improving organizational effectiveness.

- How to initiate organizational improvement at the Mega, Macro, or Micro levels.

- Strategic planning: The 12 steps for doing it, and the four major areas it covers: Scoping, data collecting, planning, implementation, and evaluation.

- Reactive vs. proactive needs assessment.

- When strategic planning is most powerful (starting at the Mega level).

- How to do strategic planning: Rolling-up, rolling-down, or both.

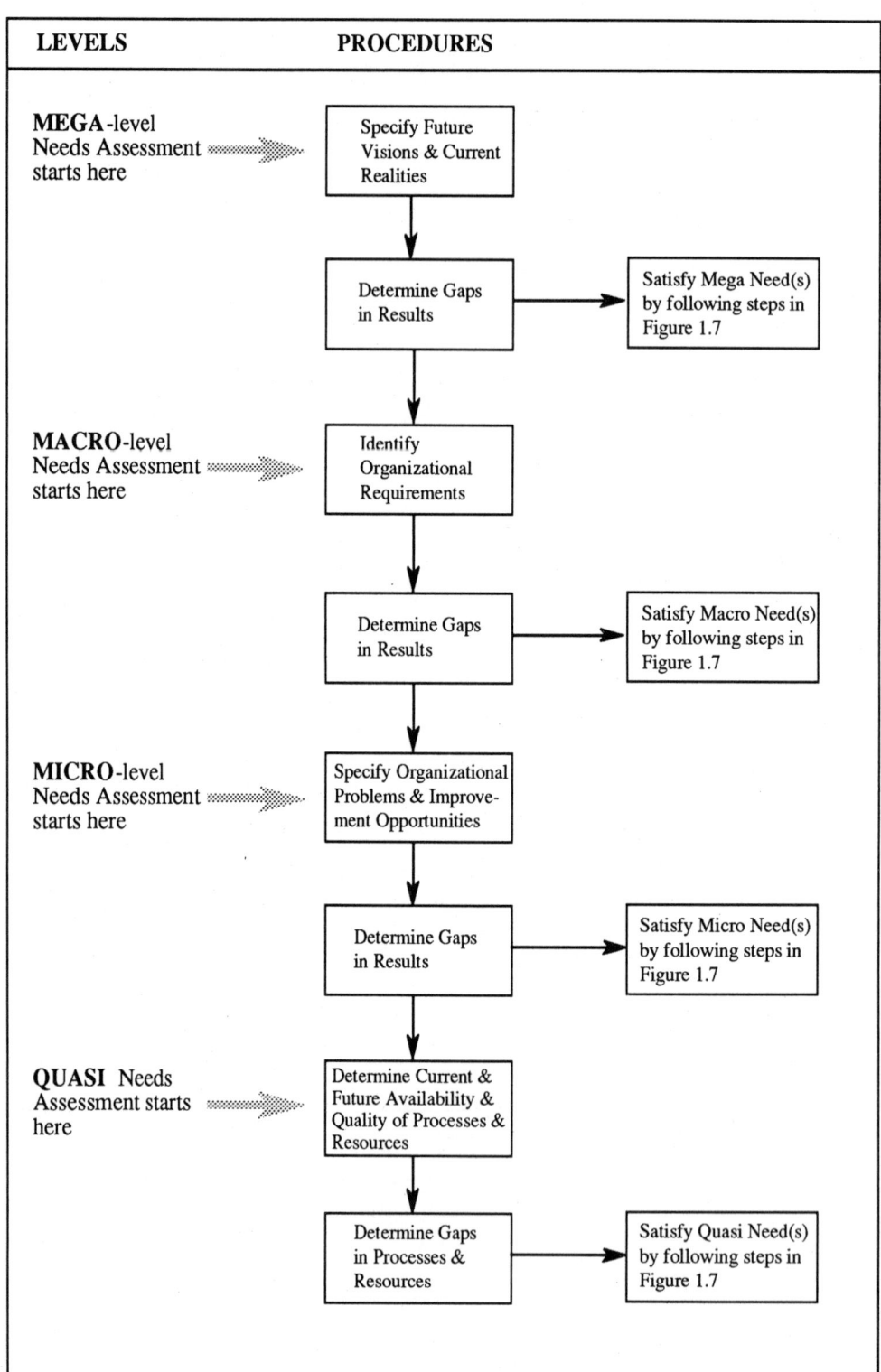

A guide to follow when conducting needs assessment at Mega, Macro, and Micro levels, and when identifying Quasi Needs.

Relating Needs Assessment, Organizational Effectiveness, and Strategic Planning

Organizational effectiveness relates to the usefulness of what an organization (i.e., corporation, company, educational agency) uses, does, and delivers to individuals and groups within the organization, to the organization itself, and to the organization's external clients and stakeholders who may benefit from effective organizational performance. One can be effective at the following levels:

- **The Micro level:** An individual or small group of workers and the *products* they deliver to other individual workers within the organization (such as fabric woven at one work station is seamed at another; computer training completers become inputs for the Total Quality Management trainers, etc.).
- **The Macro level:** External clients who receive the *outputs* of our organization (such as a delivered over-the-counter drug; delivered computer systems; delivered consulting services).
- **The Mega level:** The usefulness, or *outcome* (including safety, health, quality of life indicators) of the outputs for both the client and the society (such as safe, low-cost nuclear power; safe automobiles; crude oil delivered to a refinery without spills and pollution).

Where should your organization be headed? Effective for whom?

All organizations have a purpose. As we noted in Chapter 1, posing the right questions will provide you the opportunity to change direction, reaffirm your goals, or make mid-course corrections. Needs assessments are critical tools in planning: Based on finding the gaps between current and desired results, you may plan to continue what you started doing, or change direction.

Here, again, it is important to emphasize the three critical questions (posed in Table 1.1) to ask of your organization. These questions define the level of your organizational effectiveness: they relate not only to the level of needs assessment you do, but also to determining the primary client and beneficiary of the needs assessment level you selected (see Table 6.1).

Table 6.1. Questions to be asked and answered in any needs assessment and planning effort, and each one's primary recipients and consequences.

Organizational Effectiveness Questions	Type of Needs Assessment and Planning	Primary Client and Beneficiary
Question 1. Are you concerned with the usefulness—both to external clients and society—of what your organization delivers?	MEGA	SOCIETY
Question 2. Are you concerned with the quality of what your organization delivers to external clients?	MACRO	ORGANIZATION
Question 3. Are you concerned with the quality of what is turned out within your organization and is used by internal clients?	MICRO	INDIVIDUAL or SMALL GROUP

The selection of one of the needs assessment levels, either formally or by assumption, will determine the nature of the organization's "vision" and the starting place for needs assessment and strategic planning. A Macro-level Needs Assessment will regard the company as the primary stakeholder and beneficiary. A Micro vision will optimize on one part of a total enterprise (i.e., corporation, company, or educational agency). A Mega approach will unite and integrate Macro and Micro with it in a common mission where the primary client and beneficiary are today's and tomorrow's society.

Needs assessment, planning, types of results, and the Organizational Elements Model

As we noted in Chapter 1, the levels of needs assessment, planning, and results are related as indicated in Table 6.2 (this table is the same as Table 1.4).

Table 6.2. Relating level/scope of planning and needs assessment, primary clients and beneficiaries, and the results elements of the OEM.

Level/Scope of Planning & Needs Assessment	Primary Client and Beneficiary	Organizational Elements
MEGA	Society/Community	Outcomes
MACRO	The organization itself	Outputs
MICRO	Individuals and small groups	Products

Inputs and Processes are organizational elements which relate to that which organizations use and do. Interventions are best directed towards the relationships among Outcomes, Outputs and Products, and should be considered only on the basis of making a justifiable change to at least one (if not all) of these three types of results.

A Chain of Results

Mega-, Macro-, and Micro-level results are linked. Within the Mega level are the results and payoffs from the Macro-level. Within the Macro level are the contributions of the Micro level. Effective organizations link the ends and means of all three levels (Kaufman, 1992a, b). The relationships among the three levels form a chain of results:

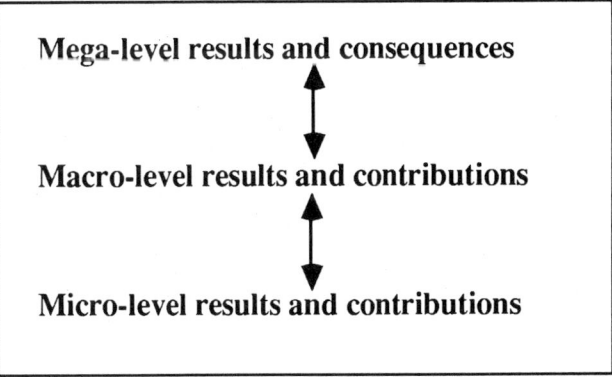

Correct application of needs assessment will allow each of the levels in this chain of results to be related to the other levels and to be mutually contributing to organizational effectiveness.

The relationship between needs assessment and strategic planning

Strategic planning is the process of finding out where your organization should be headed, what it should produce and deliver, and to whom it should be delivering outputs. Strategic planning is usually seen as developing a blueprint for creating a better future in the presence of competition and obstacles. As we will note in a moment, this is a reactive stance but not the only approach—proactive needs assessment and planning are distinct (and useful) options.

Three levels to initiate strategic planning

One may start strategic planning for any one of the client/beneficiary levels: Mega, Macro, or Micro. At a Macro level, any division or unit of the organization could be the subject of strategic planning, but such a starting place would assume that one's business unit should continue and grow. Considerations of selling, phasing out, reducing, or quitting are not probable conclusions since the mind-set here is that one's own "home" is the primary client and beneficiary. (The term "tactical" might be more accurate in this case.)

Still even narrower is the Micro level. The focus here is on an individual or a small unit of the organization (e.g., the sales department; the manufacturing vice president; shipping; processing; English Department; etc.) as the primary client. Because the perspective of Micro-level planners is not likely to include either the total organization or the society/external clients, the plan developed at this level is likely to be reactive and tending to perpetuate and nurture itself.

Planning at the Mega level will identify the kind of world—for our clients, ourselves, and our neighbors—which we want to help create. Instead of limiting ourselves to working to reduce costs, containing labor demands, reacting to economic crises, conducting damage control, or limiting our losses, this Mega level focus tends to be a proactive approach. It builds a new and improving future, not simply responding to situations. It is a take-control, shape your own future perspective. It intends to allow you to become the master of your own future, not the victim of it.

A needs assessment which assumes the vertical integration of Mega-, Macro-, and Micro-levels is a key to organizational survival and success. Figure 6.1 provides a job aid for that.

A strategic planning process: A Mega-holistic framework

There are 12 steps in the process for doing strategic planning correctly: When you use and implement these steps you will start outside the organization and move inward. The 12 steps can be grouped into four major clusters:

- Scoping.
- Data collecting.
- Planning.
- Implementation including evaluation and revision (Kaufman, 1992a).

A graphic representation of the strategic planning process is presented in Figure 6.2. The steps within each cluster are:

Scoping

1. Select the level of strategic planning from among three alternative frames of reference: Mega, Macro, or Micro. (We urge you to choose the Mega level.)

Data Collecting

2. Identify ideal vision.
3. Identify beliefs and values of planning partners (internal and external clients, society).
4. Identify current missions (and put them in performance/results terms).
5. Identify needs (as gaps between current results and desired—even ideal—ones).

Planning

6. Identify matches and mismatches: integrating visions, beliefs, needs, and current missions.
7. Reconcile differences.

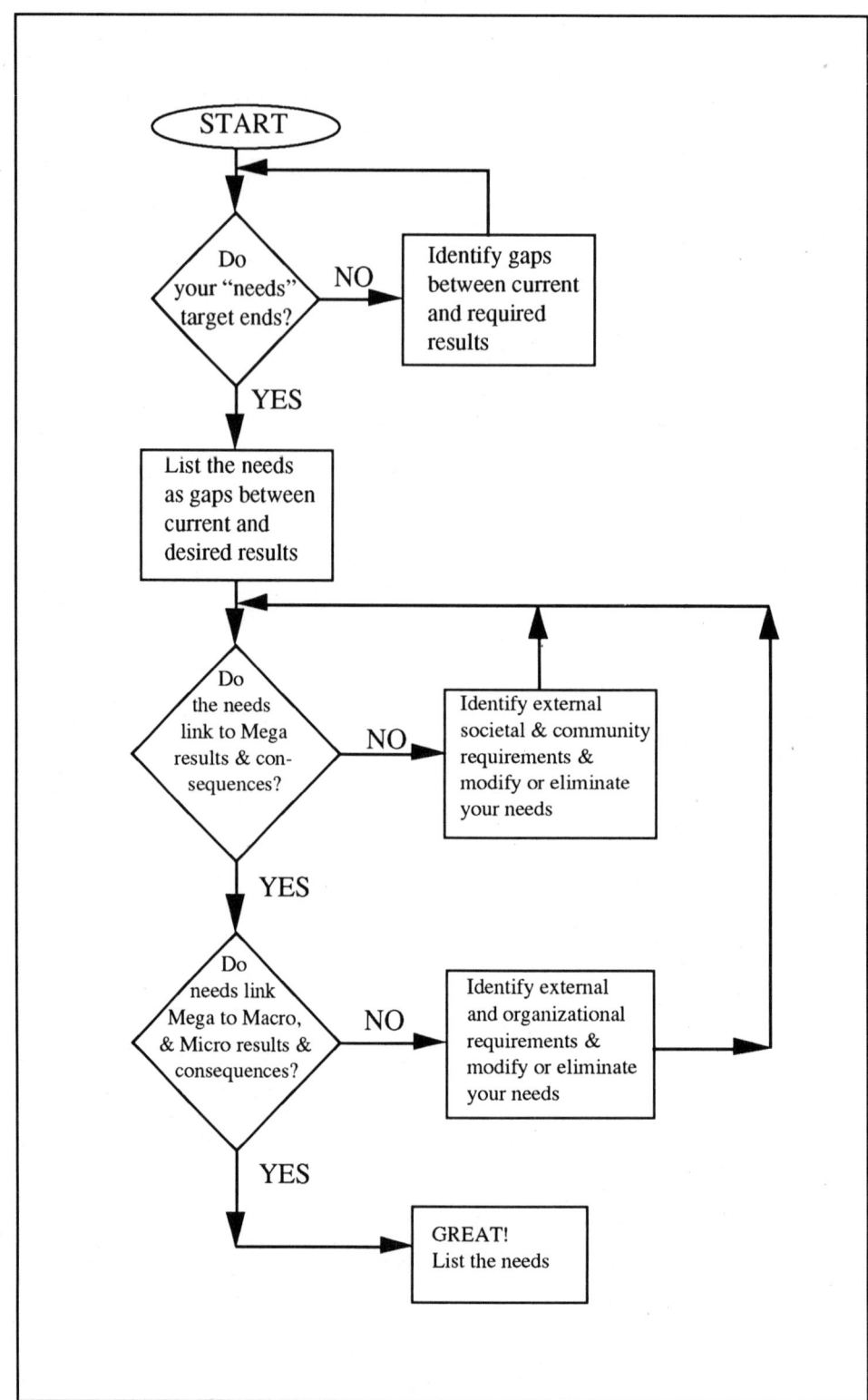

Figure 6.1. An algorithm for relating needs to gaps in results and also assuring that they link all three levels of results.

8. Select long- and short-term mission objectives (building blocks toward the ideal vision).
9. Identify SWOTs—Strengths, Weaknesses, Opportunities, and Threats.
10. Derive decision rules (results-oriented policies).
11. Develop strategic action plans.

Implementation and Evaluation

12. Put the strategic plan to work, evaluate it in operation, and revise when and as required.

Because this framework encourages including the Mega-level perspective, it is called "Strategic Planning Plus" (Kaufman, 1992a).

The role and function of needs assessment in strategic planning and organizational effectiveness

Needs assessment is part of the "data collection" portion of strategic planning. Its contribution is in steps 5, 6, and 7:

(5) Identify needs (as gaps between current results and desired ones).
(6) Identify matches and mismatches: integrating visions, beliefs, needs, and current missions.
(7) Reconcile differences.

In this context, needs assessment serves to provide solid, justifiable results focused determination of "where we are now" and "where we should be." It provides the data to transition from scope and vision to implementation and results.

If organizations are to be effective, they must not only look at problems that are already upon them, but also look to possible opportunities. Therefore, needs assessments and planning may be reactive, proactive, or both.

NEEDS ASSESSMENT & ORGANIZATIONAL EFFECTIVENESS—CHAPTER 6

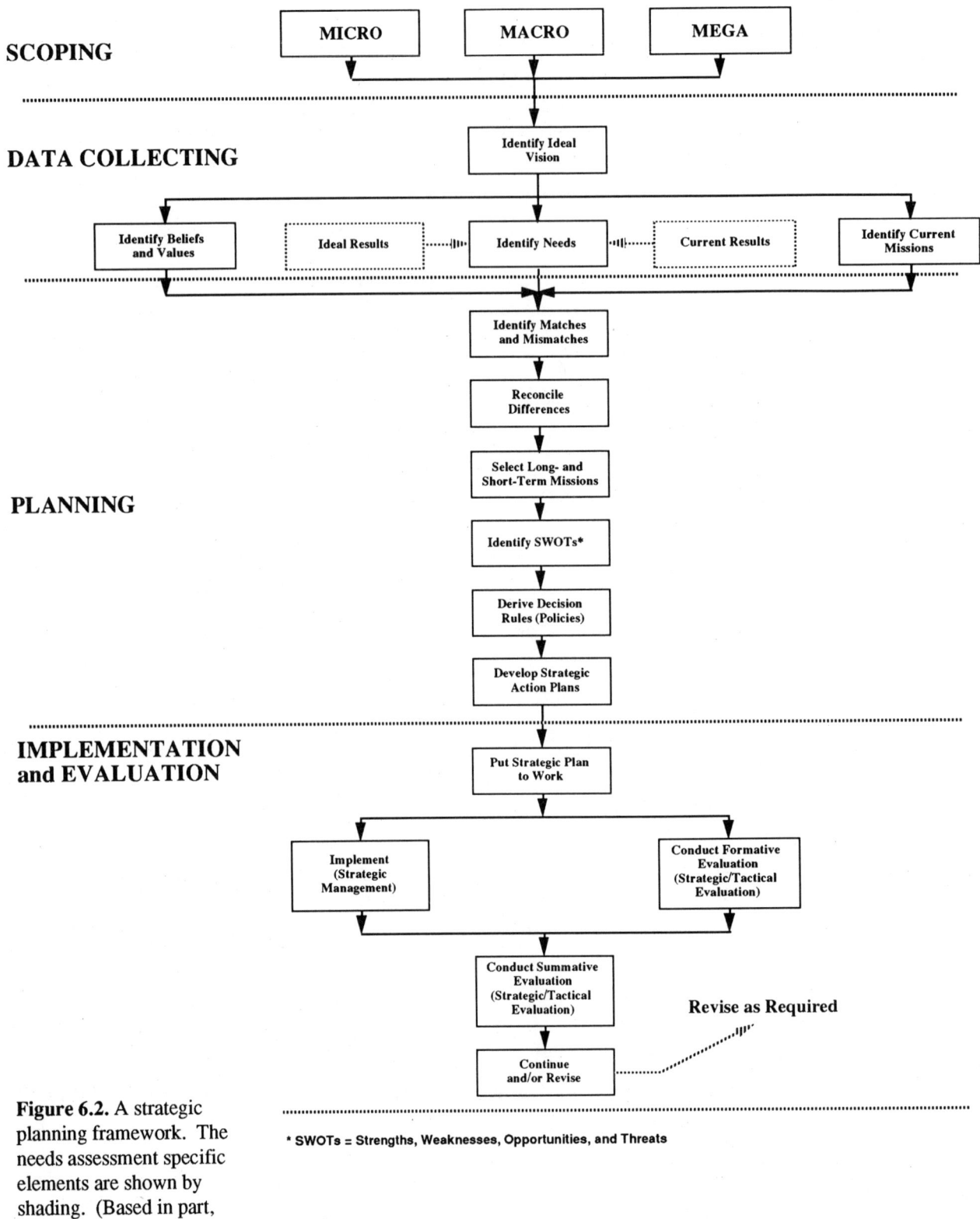

Figure 6.2. A strategic planning framework. The needs assessment specific elements are shown by shading. (Based in part, on Kaufman, 1992a.)

* SWOTs = Strengths, Weaknesses, Opportunities, and Threats

Reactive and proactive planning

A major "key" in defining and achieving organizational effectiveness is the orientation to the clients and beneficiaries of the organization. One orientation is to react to situations and problems and "fix" them as you can, and the other is to seek change before being overcome by events. Because needs assessment activities are so often initiated by people who do not yet understand the importance of a holistic approach, the following might help in developing better understanding.

Reactive planning. Needs assessment and planning are often initiated in a reactive mode because they respond to the pressures of competition, obstacles, a changing world, political influences, business environment, or resource shifts. Conventional wisdom has the planners strive to maintain a "market focus" while attempting to create a more successful organization within the limits of present corporate philosophy and mission. Reactive approaches are not likely to challenge the preeminence of their own organization, create new businesses, or shut down faltering ones.

Being "market driven" may simply mean "give 'em what they want" or it could result in identifying the joint arena shared by (a) what the client wants, (b) what one's organization can deliver, (c) what the client should have, and (d) what the external world should have. Unfortunately, many interpret "market driven" only in terms of (a) and (b) and end up in a very short-run position. When one is in a reactive mode, options (a) and (b) seem to take center-stage, while a more caring and responsible proactive mode will result in (a), (b), (c), and (d) being attended to. Before assuming that client satisfaction—that which "drives" conventional market-driven approaches as well as Total Quality Management approaches (see Chapter 3)—recall that there have been many outputs which customers really liked, but were not very satisfactory from a Mega-level perspective: e.g., plastics which don't bio-degrade, asbestos insulation, cigarettes, marbled beef....

Proactive planning. Another (and more unusual) reason to do planning and needs assessment is to become proactive: to create something new and/or change things **before** there are pressures, crises, and problems. The proactive approach resonates to Drucker's advice that doing the right job is more important than doing the job right.

One may conduct any of the three types of planning in either a reactive or proactive mode, or do both at the same time.

Strategic thinking

A most important contribution of strategic planning and needs assessment is not any plan but actually **thinking strategically**...the way the organizational partners go about identifying and dealing with the future and survival, opportunities, and threats. Strategic thinking can be proactive and is revealed by a switch from dealing with one's organization as a splintered aggregate of fragmented parts (and employees) competing for resources, to considering one's organization as an integrated system where each part effectively and efficiently contributes to the whole based on agreed upon and mutually rewarding visions. Strategic thinking involves a shift from linear, lock-stepped, authoritarian, means-process-only oriented, budget-driven tactics to a future-oriented frame of reference where means are selected on the basis of mutually rewarding ends. Strategic thinking relates organizational means and products to societally useful ends.

Plans and interventions should provide proactive and societally benefitting payoffs. The primary client should be society, now and in the future. The strategies and tactics which derive from Mega-level plans will give direction for detailed planning, action, evaluation, and responsive change.

Improving organizational effectiveness: Starting from the bottom and working up or starting from the top and working down or both

Rolling-up/rolling-down are two approaches to needs assessment and planning.

Rolling-up. In customary planning efforts, where we are headed is pre-specified, assumed, or mandated (e.g., build a bridge, design a truck, recover oil, widen a road, teach math, win a championship, develop electronic signal detection equipment). It starts with the here-and-now and simply plans to get from where we are to a specific destination. Consideration of alternative destinations (or opportunities) is not formally envisioned. Figure 6.3 shows a rolling-up sequence.

When we don't question our destinations, we build from the bottom-up. One electronics giant developed a whole array of very clever, very well-engineered consumer products. They designed, developed, set up marketing mechanisms, only to find out that they were "customerless products"—nobody could find a use for them so they didn't buy. Strangely, most

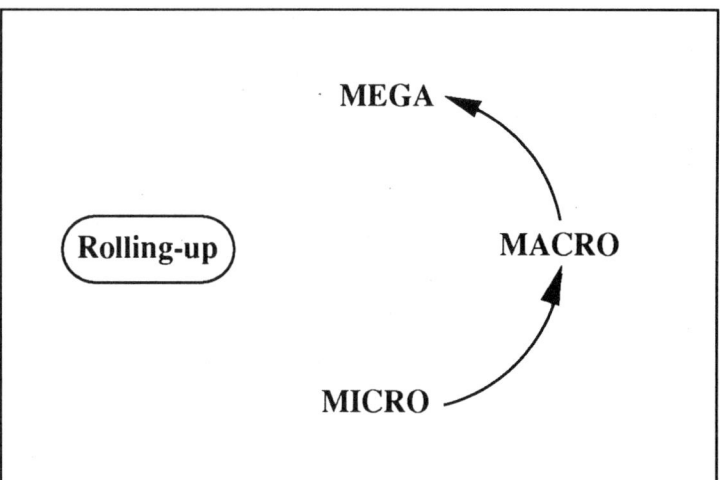

Figure 6.3. A rolling-up sequence.

planning models and approaches move in this way...they move from "good ideas" or known products and try to find a market. But this isn't the only choice.

Imagine this scenario. The skipper of a submarine looks through the periscope and announces over the intercom:

> "I now see the horizon and am ready to set our course. I want each of you to identify what it is you do and deliver...how many knots we can make both below and above surface; how long we can stay submerged, how we can maintain communication with headquarters.... Next, I want you to examine your objectives, opportunities, and threats, and then give me the strategic plan for your unit. Then, I want a special group of you to 'roll-up' your plans and develop a strategic plan for all of us. We will make up plans from your bottom-up knowledge and activities."

Silly? Of course, the sailors in the engine room, like those at the torpedo tubes and in the galley, cannot see where to go or what is on the horizon. They cannot even see each other. Those working in the innards of the ship can only provide information about their subsystem, but they cannot be expected to provide sensible overall direction.

Using this typical rolling-up sequential tactic, each operational unit, then section, then department, then division is asked, in turn, to do their "strategic plan" and these are used to build the levels above. In sequential fashion, the whole array of individual strategic plans are "rolled up" together to fashion the total organizational strategic plan.

Rolling-down. Direction flows downward, information up. It isn't that lower-level workers don't have the latent capacity to be the skipper, and it isn't that their dedication to the mission isn't necessary. The fact is that the whole is more than the sum of the parts, and the aggregate has to take into account more than the reactive rolling-up of all of the parts of the organization.

Uncommon is the approach which defines the external—outside the organization—environment and human condition to be achieved and then derives, moving downward (like captain to crew), that which each part of the organization must contribute. Then, each contributor may select the ways in which to cooperatively and mutually contribute to the collective mission. Planning using this tactic might move from citizens who are to be healthy down to the practices and procedures of hospital location and patient intake; from the demands of a free society, to a crude oil well head, to the deposits of oil, to extraction, distribution, and refining; from fast, safe, low-polluting, economical transportation of people over long distances, to the design of a specific vehicle, to the development, manufacturing, quality assurance, delivery, and profitable use. Figure 6.4 shows a rolling-down sequence.

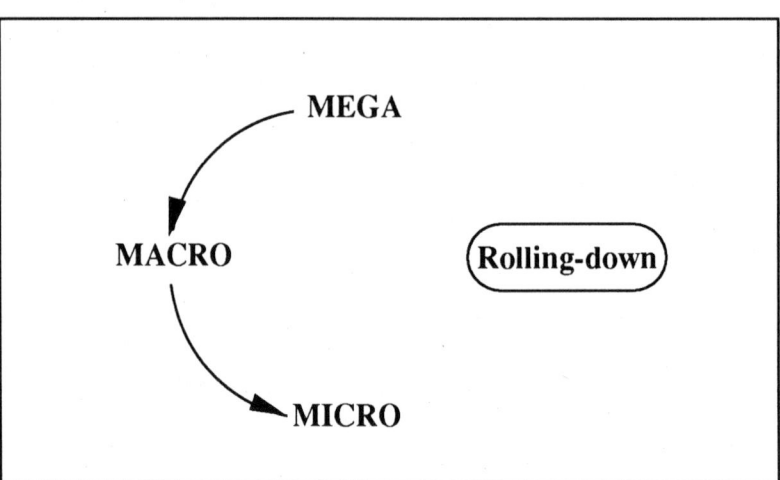

Figure 6.4. A rolling-down sequence.

Thus, needs assessment and strategic planning can start at the top by considering future opportunities and possibilities and developing a responsive system downward. Or it can start at the bottom and take the plans and products for each operating entity and roll them all up to a plan for the total organization. How you progress—starting at the bottom or the top—may determine what ends you get.

Rolling-down/rolling-up: an integrated approach. Most organizations are currently successful in the things they already do and deliver. They should continue that which is successful while also seeking what to change, modify, add, delete, or acquire. It is not probable (and possible) that an entirely new organization might be created and the existing one sold, disbanded, or moth-balled. It is reasonable to both roll-up and roll-down planning simultaneously, compare the results from both the inside-out and outside-in perspective, and revise as required: develop the up-from-the-bottom strategic plan and, at the same time (ideally independently), develop the down-from-the-top plan and see if they meet and match! An integrated sequence is shown in Figure 6.5.

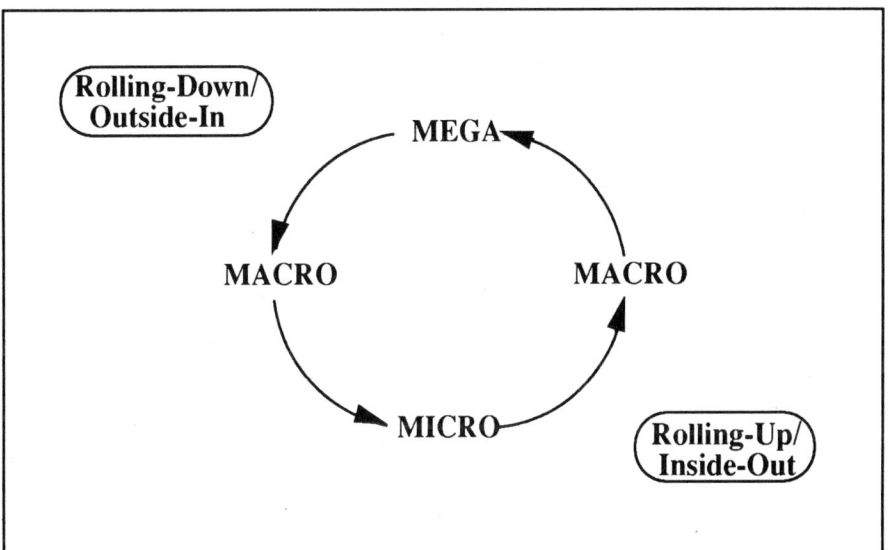

Figure 6.5. Rolling-down/rolling-up: an integrated approach.

If there are mismatches between elements of the two plans—rolling-down and rolling-up—then changes should be made.

By using both approaches you and your organization might get the best of all possible worlds by using both a proactive and reactive mode to identify a useful future for all concerned.

Chapter Summary

Any intentional effort to improve organizational and/or individual effectiveness (including the use of needs assessment and strategic planning) should ask and answer important questions concerning who are the primary clients and beneficiaries of that which is planned and ultimately delivered—who gets improved effectiveness?

- The society and stakeholders (Mega level)?
- The organization itself (Macro level)?
- An individual or small group within the company (Micro level)?

The Mega level—the society and external stakeholders—focus is encouraged as both practical and imperative. In fact, the Mega level includes the Macro and Micro clients and beneficiaries.

Two alternative approaches to planning for organizational effectiveness are possible. One, primarily reactive, sequentially rolls-up the plans from the smallest units until each layer or level has been considered in a total plan. Another tactic is to sequentially "roll-down" from an identified (best, "ideal") vision to a measurable mission objective to a definition of what each possible operating entity must do and contribute to the entire enterprise. The roll-down approach is proactive and has the greater possibility of identifying new businesses and modifying existing ones. When used together, you may identify what to keep and what to change when dealing with an ongoing operation.

A strategic planning process may be seen as having four major clusters: Scoping, Data Collecting, Planning, and Implementation and Evaluation. A framework for strategic planning includes twelve steps and moves from defining one's frame of reference (Mega, Macro, Micro) and values and beliefs to needs and requirements, and then develops a strategic plan based upon the future of the organization that its partners choose to create. Needs assessment is a vital part of strategic planning...it deals with identifying and justifying the gaps between current results and desired ones, and placing the gaps in priority order.

References and Suggested Readings

Drucker, P. F. (1973) *Management: Tasks, responsibilities, practices.* New York: Harper & Row.

Kaufman, R. (1992a) *Strategic planning plus: An organizational guide.* Newbury Park, CA: Sage Publishing.

Kaufman, R. (1992b) *Mapping educational success.* Newbury Park, CA: Corwin Press, Division of Sage.

Kaufman, R. & Herman, J. (1991) *Strategic planning in education: Rethinking, restructuring, revitalizing.* Lancaster, PA: Technomic Publishing.

Ohmae, K. (1982) *The mind of the strategist: Business planning for competitive advantage.* New York: Penguin Books.

Pascale, R. T. & Athos, A. G. (1981) *The art of Japanese management: Applications for American executives.* New York: Warner.

Peters, T. (1987) *Thriving on chaos: Handbook for a management revolution.* New York: Alfred A. Knopf.

Pfeiffer, J. W., Goodstein, L. D., & Nolan, T. M. (1989) *Shaping strategic planning: Frogs, bees, and turkey tails.* Glenview, IL: Scott, Foresman.

Rummler, G.A. & Brache, A.P. (1990) *Improving performance: How to manage the white space on the organization chart.* San Francisco, CA: Jossey-Bass.

A NEEDS ASSESSMENT TOOL KIT

Chapter 7

Following are tools and techniques which may be useful when doing a needs assessment. Each needs assessment application is at least a bit different, so knowing the basic concepts and tools will be useful as you tailor them for each situation.

We both repeat some of the needs assessment tools, forms, and job aids from earlier chapters here, as well as add some more for specific applications.

How to "Market" Needs Assessment

Here are some questions and issues you might face—and how to respond.

You define "need" and "needs assessment" differently from many others. How do I convince others that this approach is right?

It isn't a matter of right or wrong, but a question of what will get useful results and what won't. Bullying and directly attacking others won't be productive. Help others understand what you know, can do, will contribute, and help them see the payoffs for defining and applying needs assessment "our way."

Several means for changing minds are possible:

> *Shifting from using (and thinking) "need" as a verb to "need" as noun—a gap in results.*

> When someone uses "needs" as a verb, such as "we 'need' training," "we 'need' more computer literate people," ask them:

>> "If we completed successful training, what would be the result?" Or "What would be the consequence of almost everyone being computer literate?"

> Keep, gently, asking what consequences and payoffs would result until you agree on the ends to be accomplished. Then, with a shared destination, you can plot the gaps between current results and payoffs and desired ones. The following job aid (see Figure 7.1) can be useful.

> *Getting results criteria into needs statements, and making certain that needs statements do not prematurely identify the means and resources to be employed.*

> Objectives, to be truly useful, must identify a destination, not a process or resource. The basic elements of a useful objective state where you are going and how you can tell when you have arrived. If you include any how-to-do-it in an objective or in a need statement you risk selecting a solution, means, resource, or intervention which will not close the gap in results.

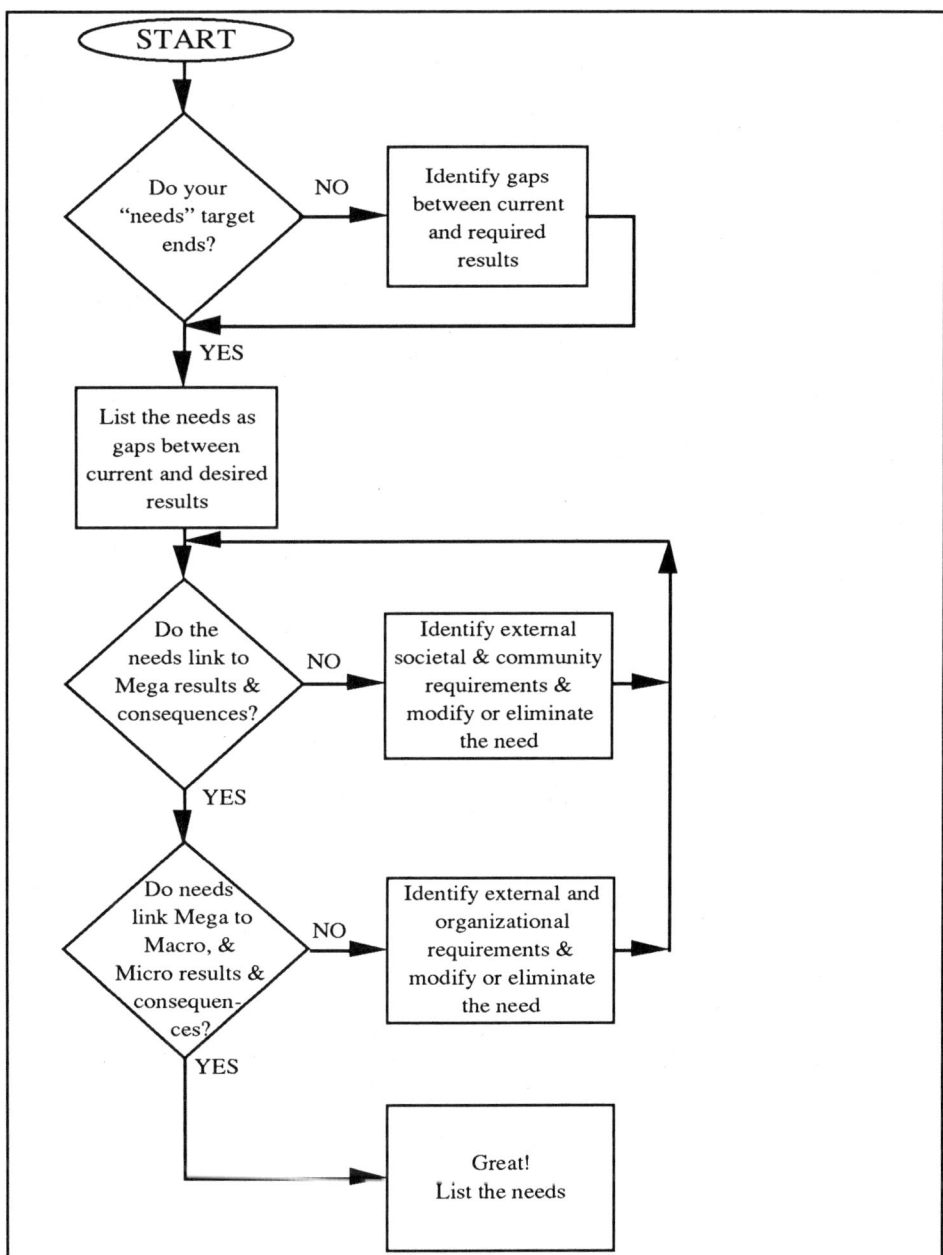

Figure 7.1. A guide for relating needs to gaps in results and also assuring that they link all three levels of results.

A useful objective will have the following elements:

- What result, performance, or consequence is to be achieved?
- Who or what will display or demonstrate that result, performance, or consequence?
- Under what condition will the result, performance, or consequence be observed?

- What criteria will we use to measure the extent to which the result, performance, or consequence has been achieved?

When working with people who want to include a means or resource in an objective, write their proposed methods, means, or resources down and say "let's hold these good ideas until later and make certain that they will really be as effective as we now think they might." Later, when doing the methods-means analysis, list it as a possible way of closing the gaps—meeting the needs—in results.

It is easy to say "Consider the entire organization and the external society—the Mega Level"—but how can a person working in a training department presume to tell the bosses about strategic objectives?

There are some old paradigms still languishing in organizations, like *the bosses-tell-us-what-to-do-and-we-better-do-it syndrome*. Fortunately, most of these paradigms are crumbling or have disappeared.

One disintegrating paradigm is that bosses set directions, workers get everyone to the destinations. Total quality management (and its variations) are showing the way to developing shared visions and missions, with everyone making their individual contributions. Rugged individualism within organizations is giving way to team playing and cooperative goal setting. You are not alone, and most bosses appreciate *positive* suggestions about how to improve organizational effectiveness. Don't be afraid to work in teams and to use networks.

Many new (and long overdue) initiatives are surfacing in organizations large and small. One is empowerment: everyone can and should make a contribution, and everyone is important. Empower yourself to make suggestions on how everyone can be more successful.

How can I approach the people above me and external clients with the Mega-level Needs Assessment approach?

Most new-era executives want input. Easier done than said. Most people have not even considered the array of questions specified below which every organization faces. Use these in your discussions and to help you prepare your "case."

> **Question 1**   Do you care about the impact and contribution your organization makes to external clients and society?

Question 2 Do you care about the quality of what your organization delivers to external clients?

Question 3 Do you care about the quality of what your organization delivers to internal clients?

Question 4 Do you care about the efficiency of your operation and activities?

Question 5 Do you care about the quality and availability of your human, capital, and material resources?

Question 6 Do you care about the extent to which you have reached your objectives and/or about the value and worth of your methods?

It isn't that others are not open to asking and answering these questions... most people really have not faced the reality of all of the possibilities. Nor have they confronted the risks of not dealing with them.

One way to get active participation and commitment to the target level of needs assessments (and indeed strategic planning) is to use an agreement table such as Table 7.1.

NEEDS ASSESSMENT AND STRATEGIC PLANNING AGREEMENT TABLE	Response Client Y | N	Planners Y | N
1. The total organization, as well as each facility, should contribute to a) Clients' survival, health, and well-being. b) Clients' and societal quality of life.		
2. Clients' survival, health, and well-being will be part of the organization's and each of its facilities' mission objectives.		
3. Each organizational operational function will have objectives which contribute to #1 and #2.		
4. Each job/task will have objectives which contribute to #1, #2, and #3.		
5. A Needs Assessment will identify and document any gaps in results at the operational levels of #1, #2, #3, and #4.		
6. Human resources/training requirements will be generated from the Needs identified and selected based on the results of #5.		
7. The results of #5 may recommend non-HRD/training intervention.		
8. Evaluation will use data from comparing results with objectives for #1, #2, #3, and #4.		

Table 7.1. Needs assessment and strategic planning agreement table (Kaufman, 1992a).

By asking each person—external client, internal client, and the planners/needs assessors—to commit either "Yes" or "No" to each question, they become publicly aware of the array of options, and each must respond. Notice that if any person opts for "No," they become responsible for the non-achievement of results at that level.

Try using the agreement table. It works. And it clarifies the depth and level of the needs assessment effort and contributions.

Questions to ask and answer when you do a Needs Assessment

Before starting a needs assessment we recommend that you ask and answer a series of questions to determine the level of the needs assessment to conduct. The job aid provided in Figure 7.2 will guide your decision.

You may also determine the basic questions to pursue when conducting a needs assessment (and strategic planning) by using Table 7.2.

How to determine Needs Assessment scope and procedures

A guide to use when selecting your level and checking your work was presented earlier. It is provided once again for convenient reference on page 149.

Figure 7.3 provides the relationship among Needs Assessment, Needs Analysis, Design and Development, and implementation, control, and revision.

You may use the algorithm in Figure 7.4 to conduct a needs assessment.

You may also find the algorithm presented in Figure 7.5 useful—particularly for dealing with assigned problems coming from operations, rather than from proactive planning.

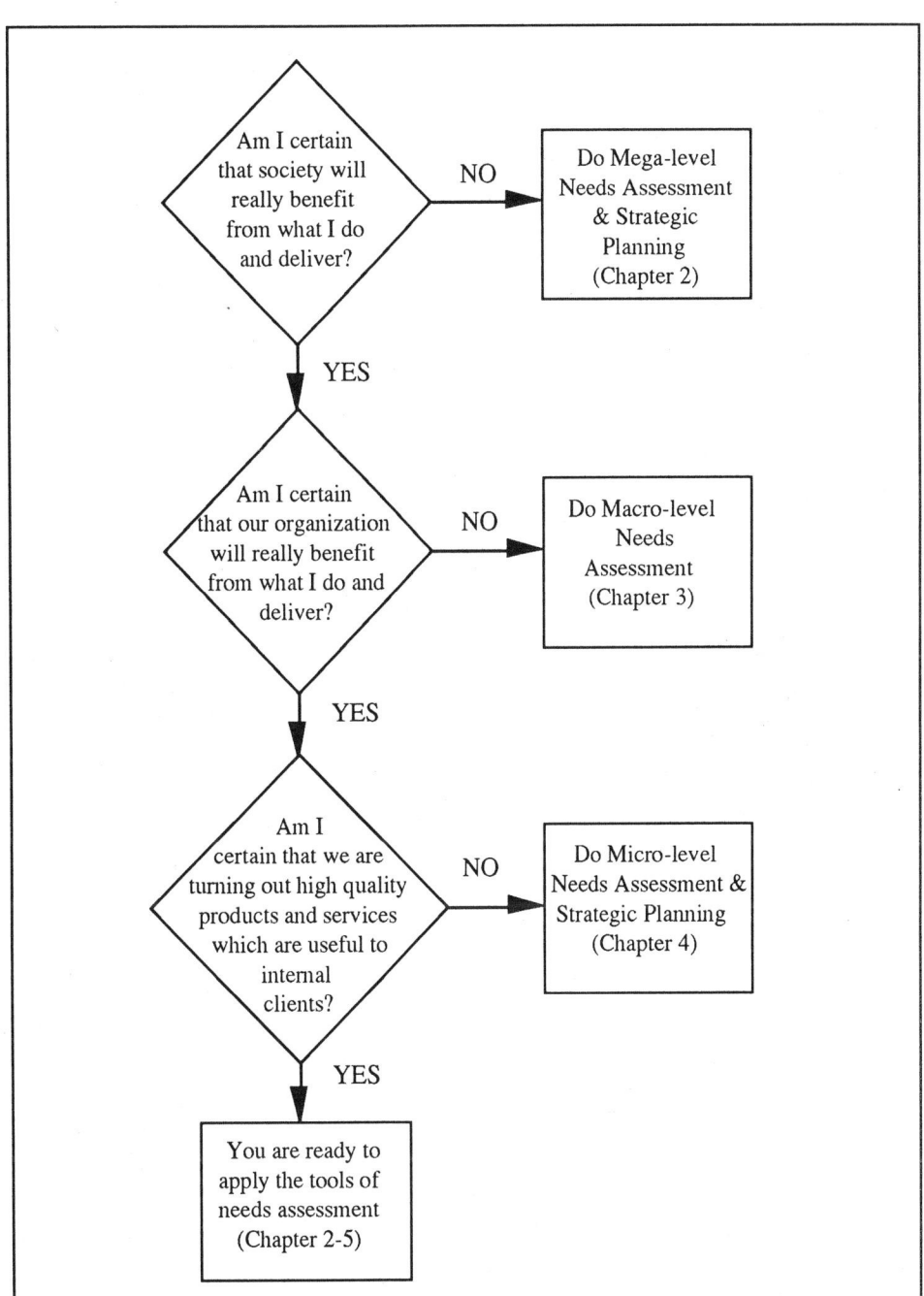

Figure 7.2. Questions to ask when selecting a Needs Assessment (and strategic planning) level.

Questions	Type of Needs Assessment						
	Level				Response		
	Mega	Macro	Micro	Quasi needs	Yes	No	I don't know
Outcome-mega oriented 1. Do you want to purposely improve our society, including measurable improvement of people's self-sufficiency, self-reliance, quality of life, and shared mutual commitment to these?	✔						
2. Are you interested in both social and economic trends as well as opportunities for the future which might not exist now or be readily apparent?	✔						
3. Are you willing to add to or delete from the current objectives of your organization?	✔						
4. Do you want to change the future and stop only reacting to the past?	✔						
Macro-related 5. Do you want to improve the current system's abilities to achieve its present purposes now and in the future?		✔					
6. Do you want to improve the output and delivery rates of the organization?		✔					
Micro-related 7. Do you want to improve on-the-job efficiency, competence, and performance levels?			✔				
Process-related 8. Do you want to help employees to be more successful in their daily efforts?				✔			
9. Do you want to improve the efficiency of working and production conditions?				✔			
Input-related 10. Do you want to improve the accountability for current organizational resources?				✔			
11. Do you want to get additional resources?				✔			

Table 7.2. Form to determine the questions to pursue when conducting Needs Assessment.

A Needs Assessment Tool Kit—Chapter 7

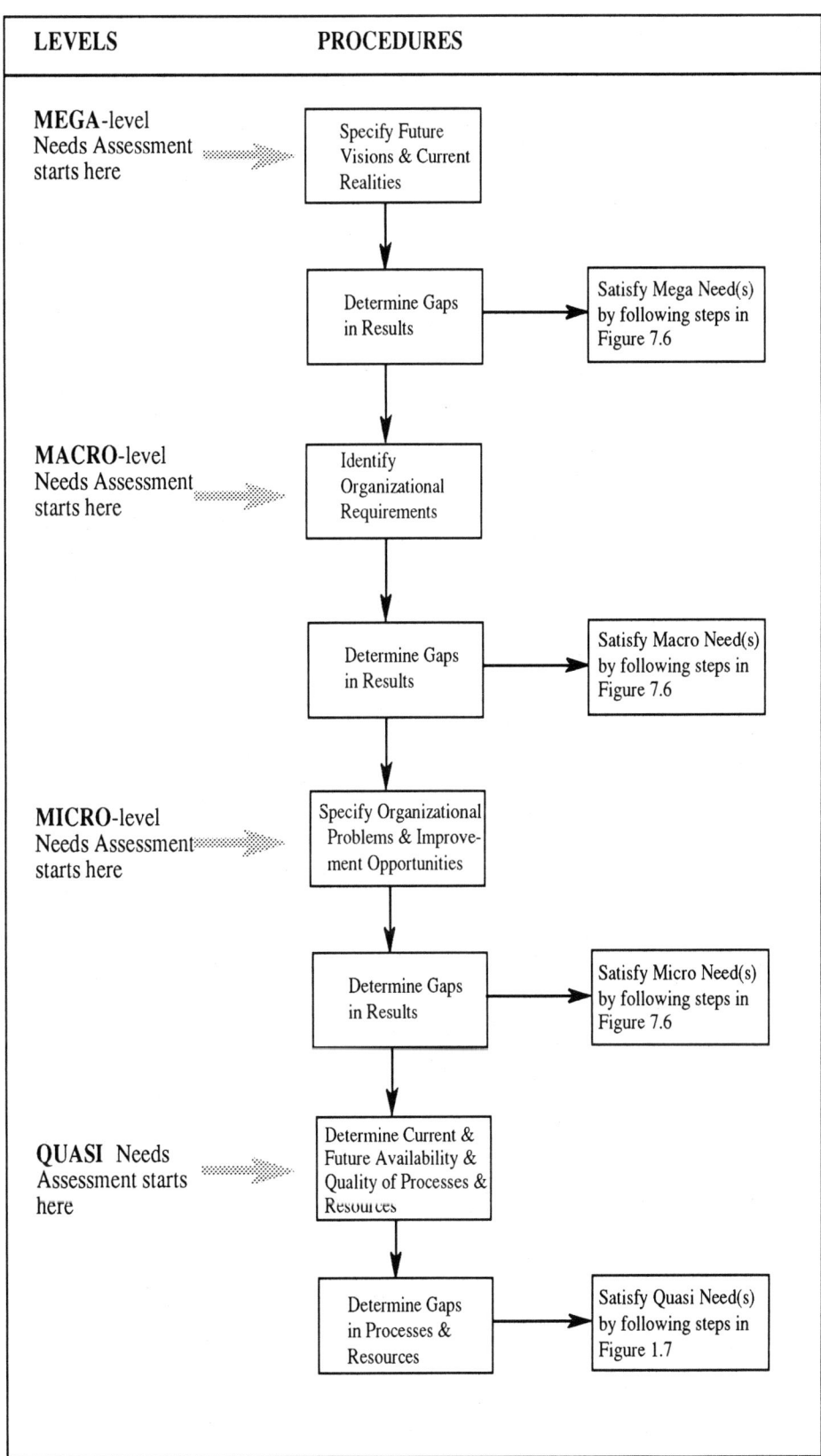

A guide to follow when conducting needs assessment at Mega, Macro, and Micro levels, and when identifying Quasi needs.

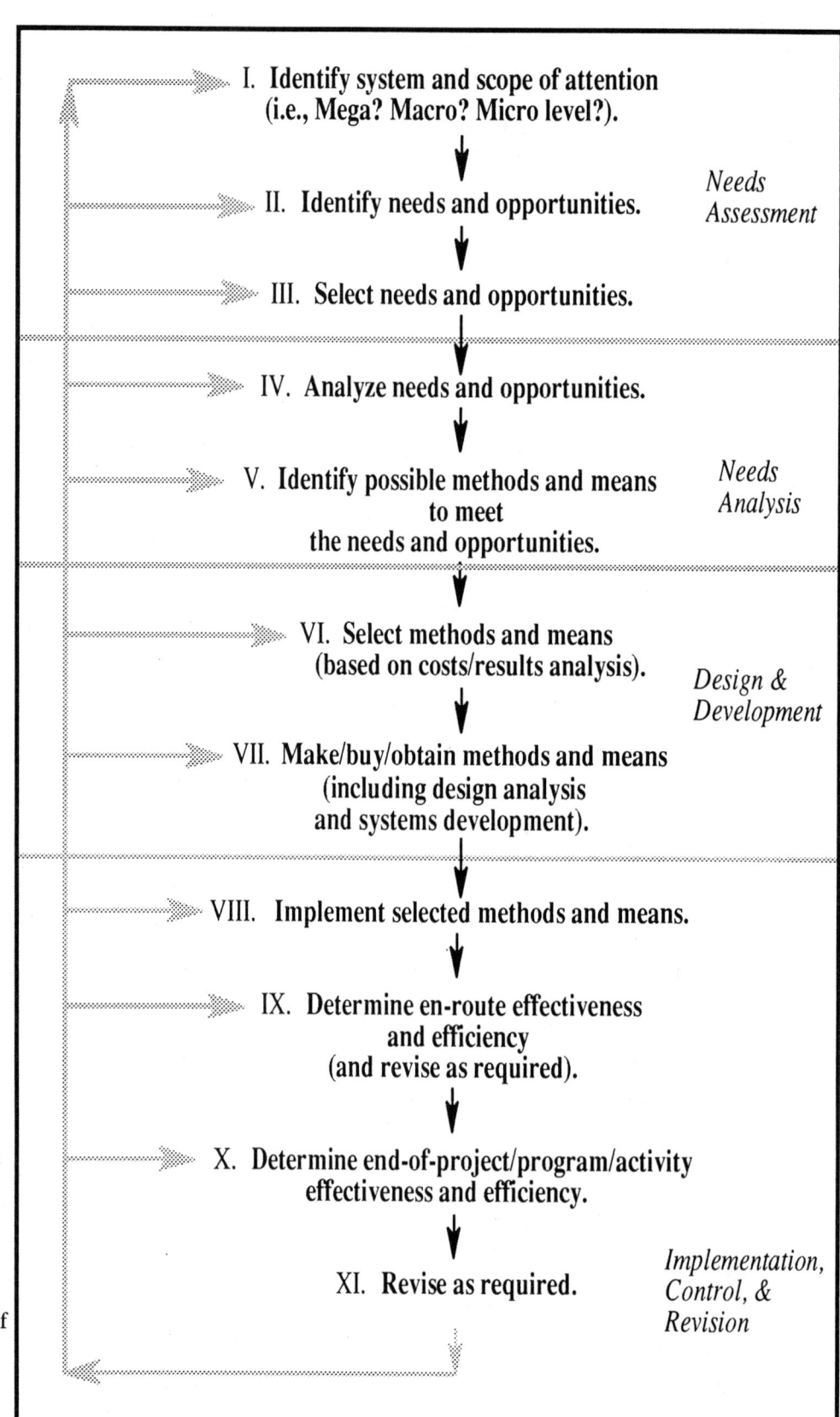

Figure 7.3. Sequence of generic needs assessment steps and their relationship to analysis, design and development, implementation and control, evaluation and revision. This sequence of steps may be applied to the different levels of needs assessment.

A NEEDS ASSESSMENT TOOL KIT—CHAPTER 7

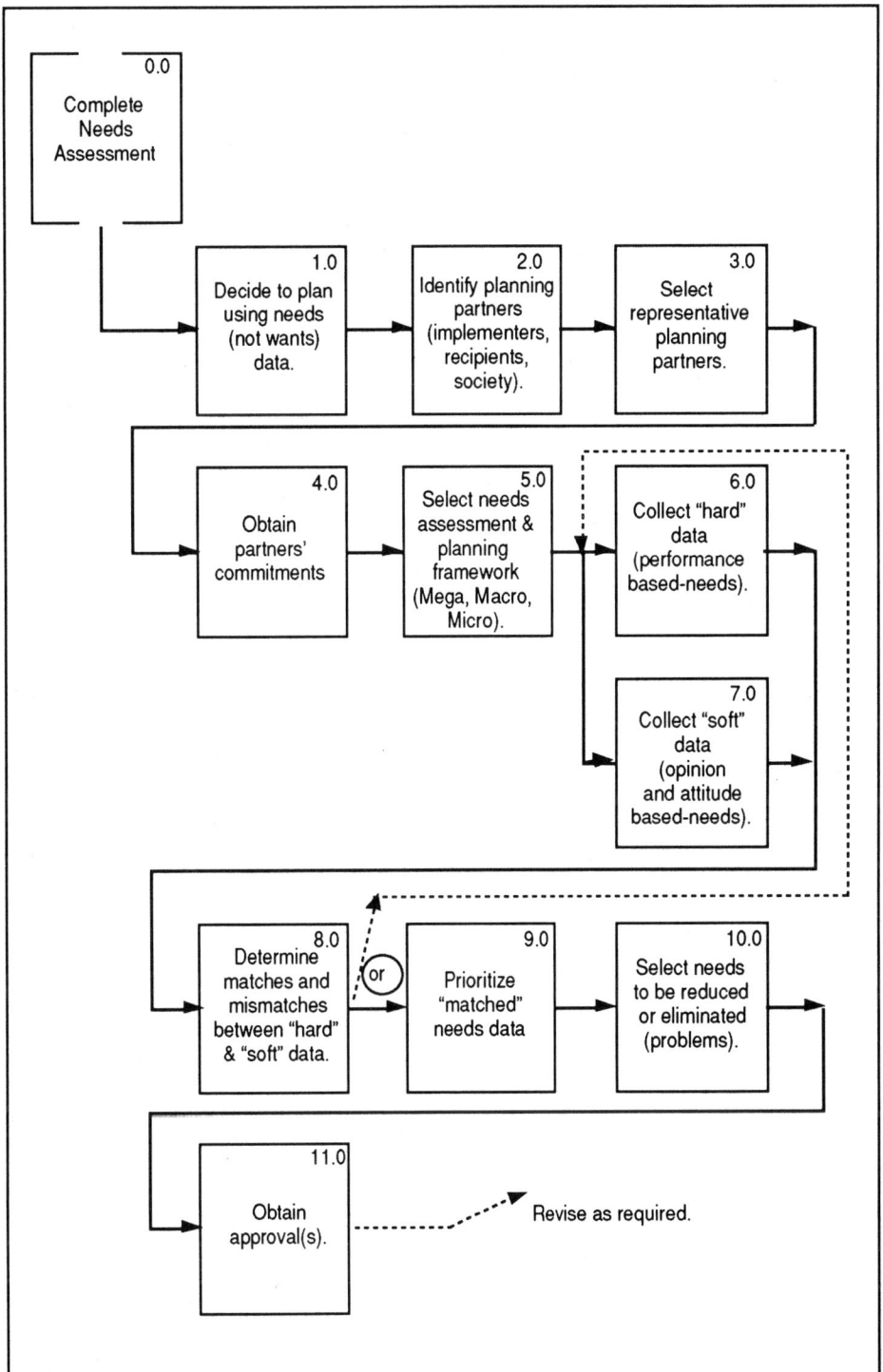

Figure 7.4. The functions required to complete a Mega-level Needs Assessment in flow chart form. Note that the functions identify only *what* is to be accomplished, not *how*. (Based on Kaumfan, 1992a.)

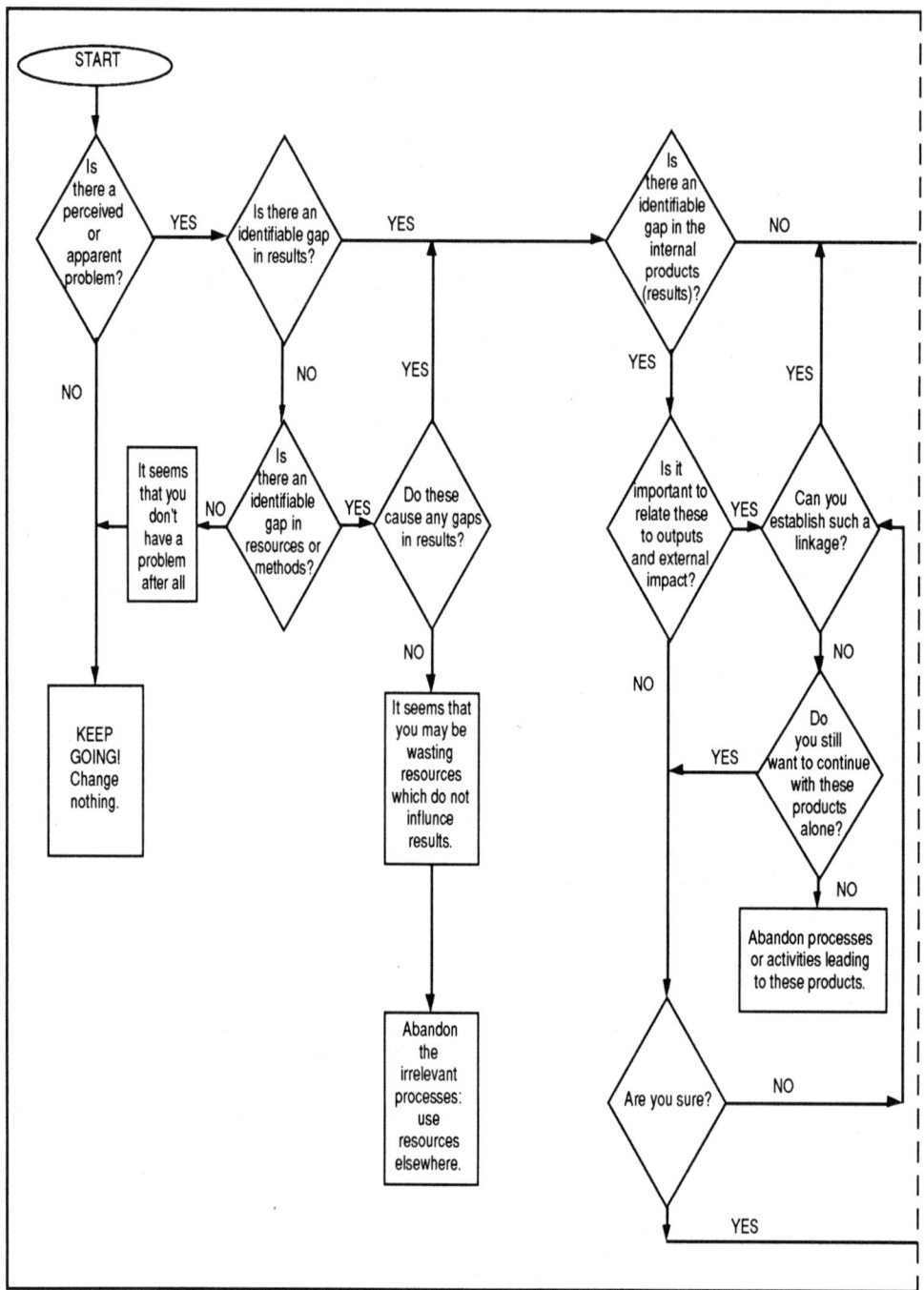

Figure 7.5. An algorithm for dealing with assigned problems which come from operation, not from proactive planning. (Based on Kaufman, 1992a, with permission.)

A Needs Assessment Tool Kit—Chapter 7

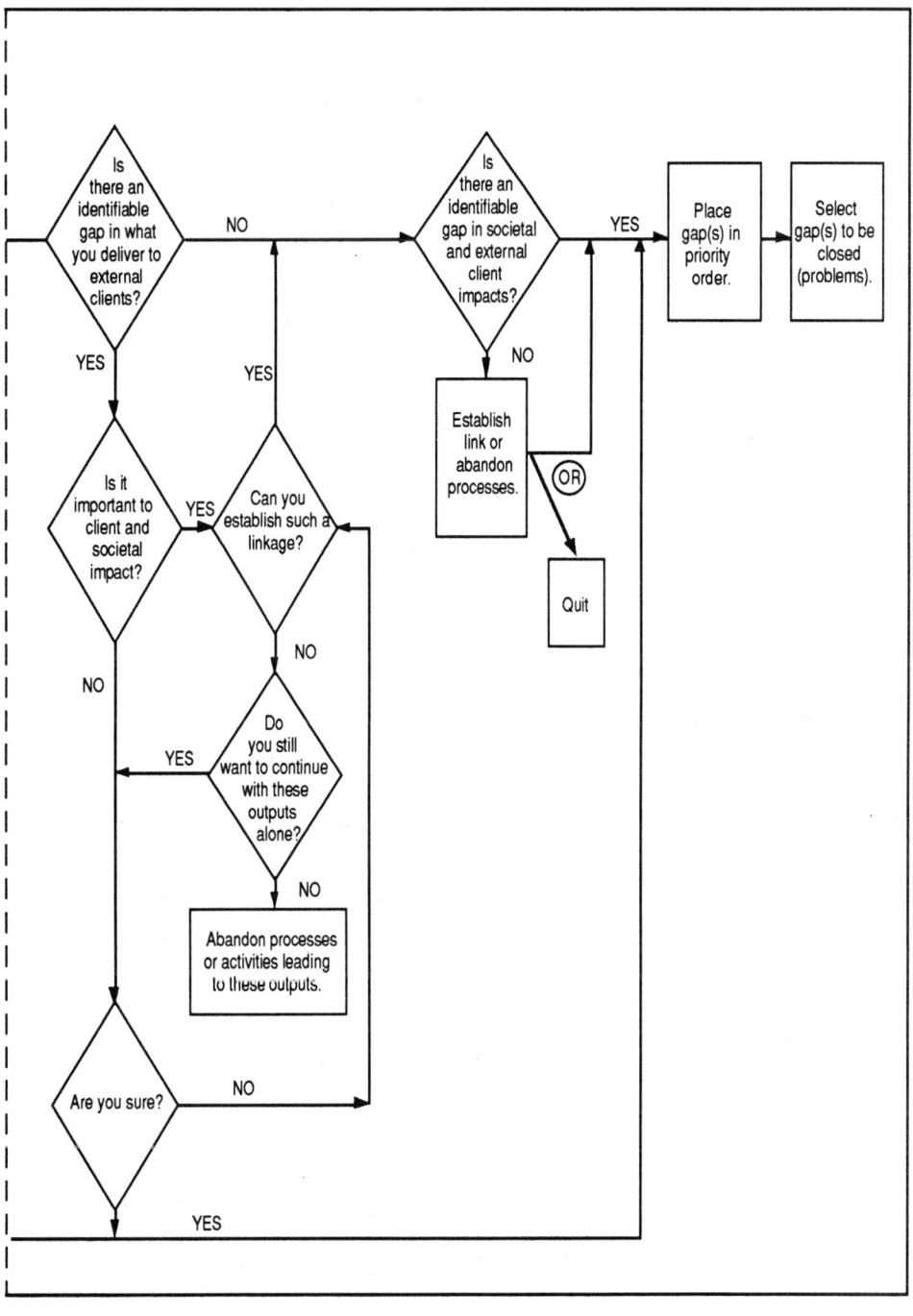

How to conduct the needs assessment at each level

Table 7.3 may be useful when identifying the different needs assessment levels.

TYPES OF RESULTS	DESCRIPTION	TYPICAL EXAMPLES
MICRO Products	Results which are building blocks for larger results	Fender, disk drive, a passed inspection or component, sale, competence obtained, etc.
MACRO Outputs	Result which can be, or is, delivered outside to society; quality of contributions	Automobile, delivered service, discharged patient, new patient, graduate, etc.
MEGA Outcomes	The social impact and payoffs of results	Continuing profit, clean environment, repeat sales, positive corporate image, self-sufficiency, etc.

Table 7.3. Three types of results, their description, and typical examples.

Mega-level Needs Assessment. You may find it useful to complete Form 7.1 when conducting a Mega-level Needs Assessment. You may also use Forms 2.1, 2.2, and 2.3 (from Chapter 2) for specific steps.

Mega-level Needs Assessment Steps	Data gathered Yes No	Comments
1. Determine your organization's ideal vision, including indicators of its impact on the survival and quality of life of its external clients and society.		
2. Determine your organization's current status with regard to its impact on clients' and society's survival and quality of life.		
3. Place Mega-level gaps (i.e., Needs) between your ideal vision and the current status, in a priority order, based on the cost to ignore vs. the cost to successfully address each identified need.		
4. Write a realistic mission objective which includes a specific sub-objective for each gap you decided to address (e.g., what you will have accomplished five or more years from now).		
5. Break down your mission objective to functional building-block objectives.		
6. Present your Mega-level needs to your clients for concurrence.		
7. List alternative methods and means for addressing your Mega-level need(s) and identify the advantages and disadvantages of each.		

Form 7.1. A checklist for recording data collection at each Mega-level Needs Assessment step.

Macro-level Needs Assessment. You may find it useful to complete the following form when conducting a Macro-level Needs Assessment. You may also use Forms 3.1, 3.2, and 3.3 (from Chapter 3) for specific steps.

Macro-level Needs Assessment Steps	Data gathered Yes / No	Comments
1. Specify the desired quality of what your organization delivers to external clients. 2. Determine the current quality of what your organization delivers to external clients. 3. List the identified, agreed upon need(s). 4. Align the needs identified at the Macro-level with the vision and mission of your organization. 5. Place Macro-level needs in a priority order, based on the cost to ignore versus the cost to address each identified need. 6. Present your Macro-level needs to your clients for concurrence. 7. List alternative methods and means for addressing your Macro-level need(s) and identify the advantages and disadvantages of each.		

Form 7.2. A checklist for recording data collection at each Macro-level Needs Assessment step.

Micro-level Needs Assessment. You may find it useful to complete Form 7.3 when conducting a Micro-level Needs Assessment. You may also use Forms 4.1, 4.2, and 4.3 (from Chapter 4).

Micro-level Needs Assessment Steps	Data gathered Yes / No	Comments
1. Determine individuals' and/or groups' required performance in terms of measurable accomplishments.		
2. Determine individuals' and/or groups' current performance status vis-a-vis the required standards established in step 1.		
3. List the identified, agreed upon Micro-level need(s).		
4. Align the needs identified at the Micro-level with the vision and mission of your organization.		
5. Place Micro-level needs in a priority order, based on the cost to ignore versus the cost to address each identified need.		
6. Present your Micro-level needs to your clients for concurrence.		
7. List alternative methods and means for addressing your Micro-level need(s) and identify the advantages and disadvantages of each.		

Form 7.3. A checklist for recording data collection at each Micro-level Needs Assessment step.

Quasi Needs Assessment. When conducting a Quasi Needs Assessment you may start at two different points. Check the steps to follow using Table 5.1 (from Chapter 5). You may find it useful to complete Form 7.4 when conducting a Quasi Needs Assessment. You may also use Forms 5.1, 5.2, and 5.3 for specific steps.

Quasi Needs Assessment Steps	Data gathered Yes / No	Comments
1. Specify the desired availability and/or quality of the organizational resources and methods.		
2. Determine the current quality and/or availability of the organizational efforts.		
3. Determine Quasi Needs—the gaps between the desired and the current organizational efforts.		
4. Align the Quasi Needs identified with the Needs at Mega, Macro, and Micro levels.		
5. Place Quasi Needs in order of importance, based on the cost to ignore versus the cost to address each identified Quasi Need(s).		
6. (or step 1 if you have already identified needs at Mega, Macro, and/or Micro levels.) Identify alternative methods and means for addressing the identified Quasi Need(s) and/or Need(s).		
7. (or step 2 if you have already identified needs at Mega, Macro, and/or Micro levels.) Identify advantages and disadvantages of each possible method and means available to get the job done.		
8. (or step 3 if you have already identified needs at Mega, Macro, and/or Micro levels.) Identify constraints and eliminate them if possible.		
9. Present alternative methods and means for addressing all agreed upon Needs and Quasi Needs to your clients, for agreement on the methods and means to be selected for action.		

Form 7.4. A checklist for recording data collection at each Quasi Needs Assessment Step.

When identifying constraints in the methods-means analysis—there are no ways and means to meet the requirement—you may use the algorithm on how to eliminate constrains presented in Figure 5.3.

Needs prioritization and linkage among different needs levels

Before listing the needs identified, determine the linkage between the needs according to the three levels: Mega, Macro, and Micro. You may use the algorithms presented in Figures 7.6 and 7.7. The results chain alignment relationships are shown in Figure 7.8.

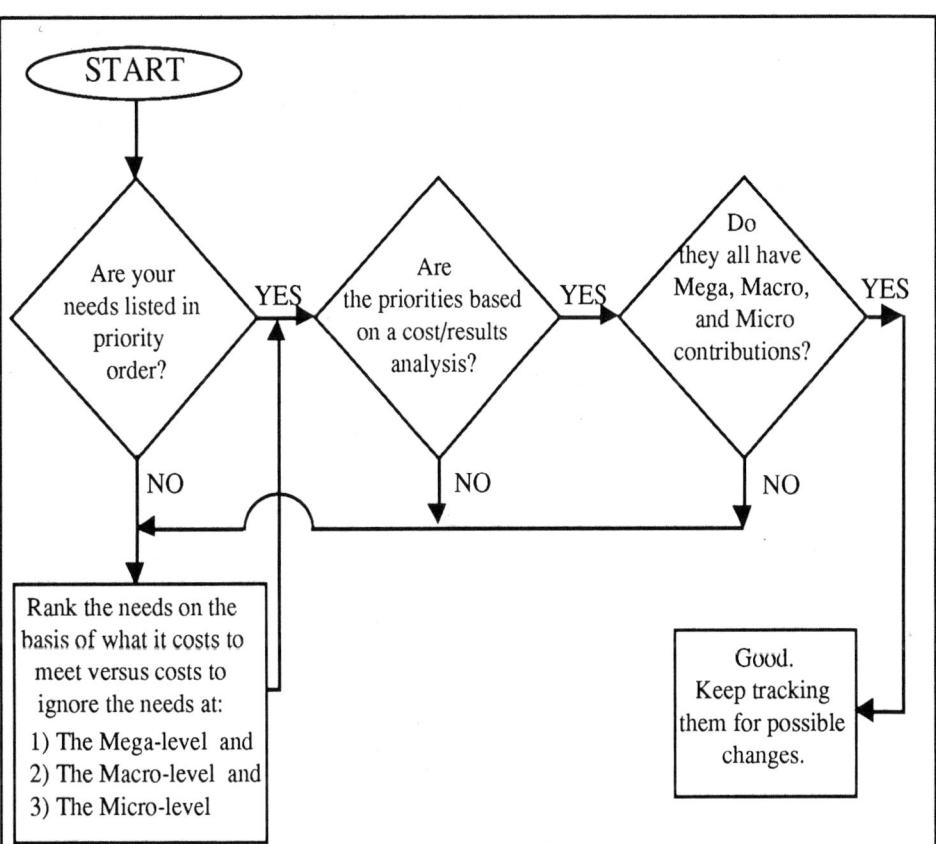

Figure 7.6. Algorithm to determine the linkage between the three levels of needs assessment. (Based on Kaufman, 1992a.)

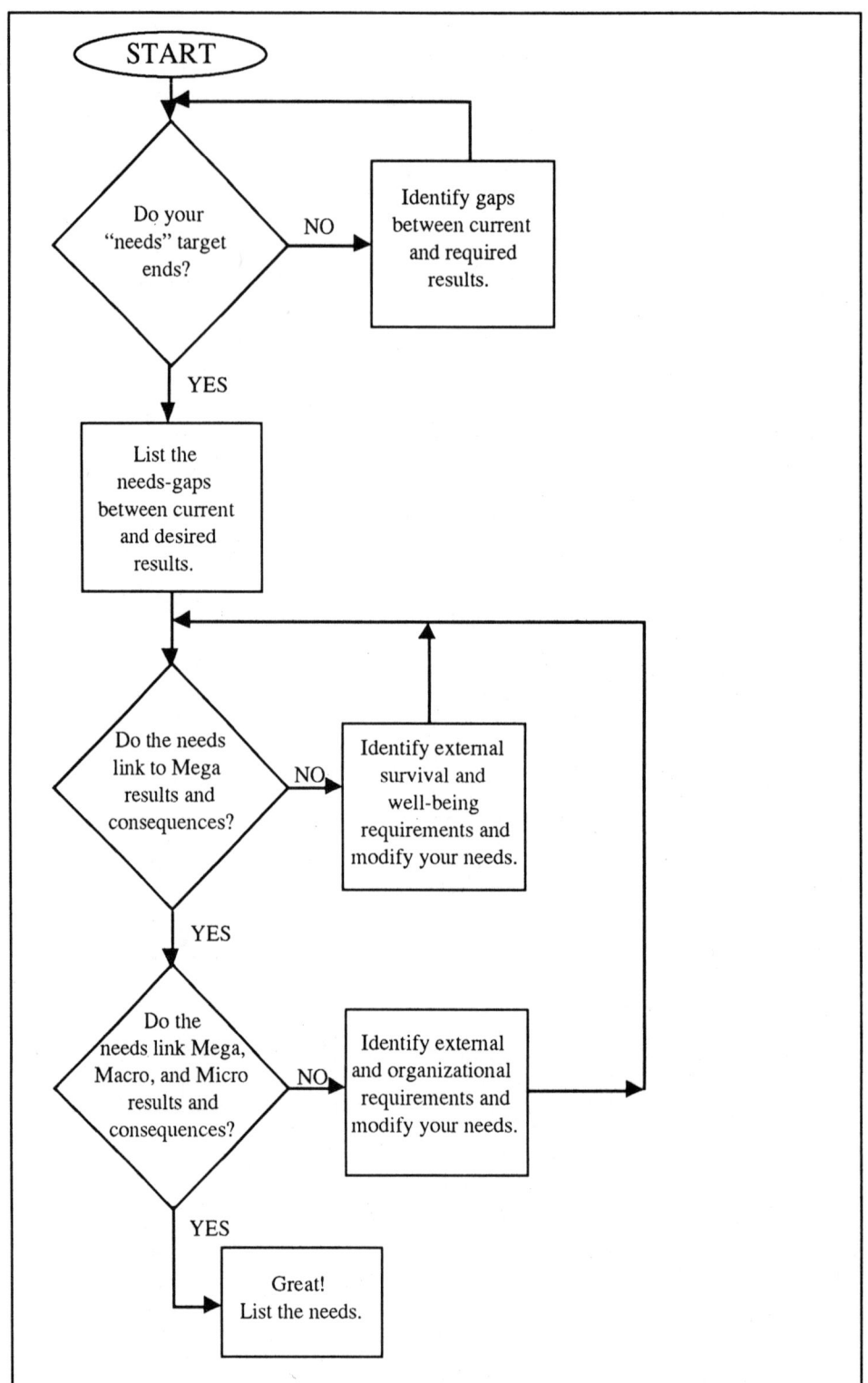

Figure 7.7. Algorithm to assure linkage between the three levels of needs assessment. (Based on Kaufman, 1992a.)

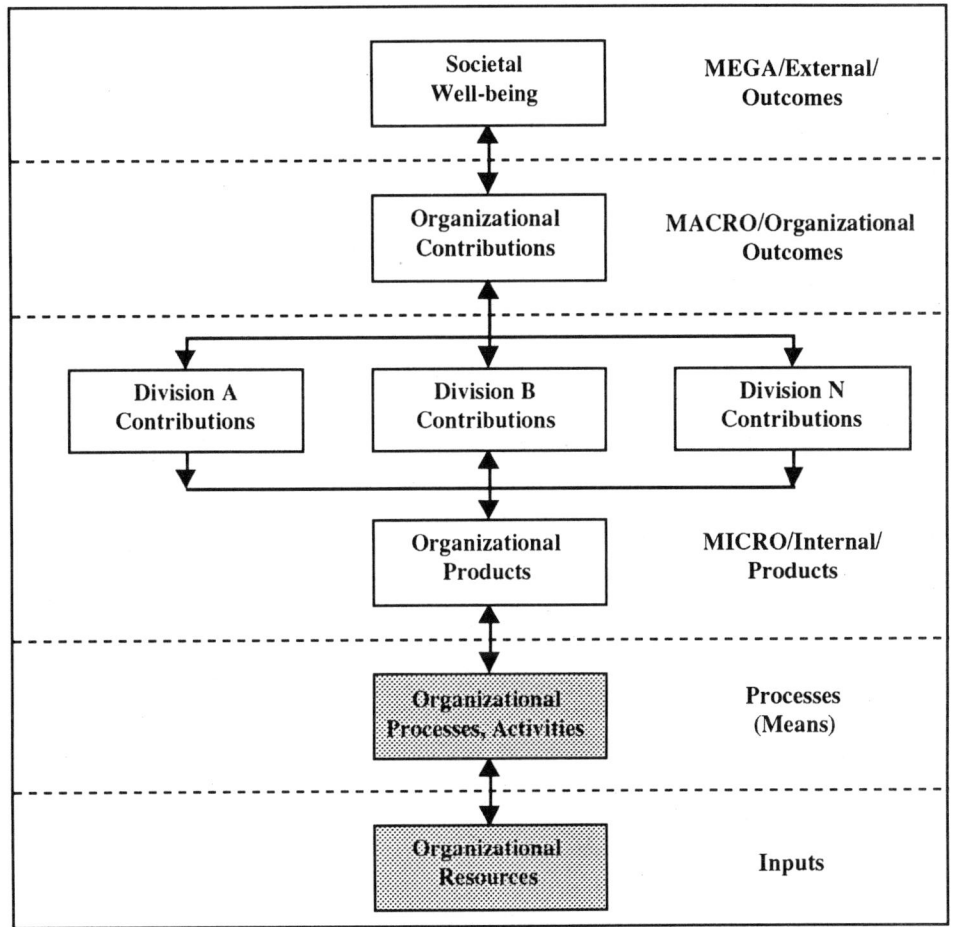

Figure 7.8. Aligning organizational resources, processes (means), products, and contributions with societal consequences.

Needs summary

After your alignment of needs at different levels, you may summarize your needs.

Here are two formats (Table 7.4 and Form 7.5) you may use. Form 7.4 is simpler; Table 7.5 (on the next page) provides greater detail for those interested in extensive needs assessment efforts.

Type of results	Current results	Desired Results
(OUTCOME) (Mega)		
OUTPUT (Macro)		
PRODUCT (Micro)		

Table 7.4. A chart for tracking the three types of results.

Identifying methods and means

After you have identified and selected the needs, you next identify possible methods-means for eliminating or reducing the gaps. A methods-means form to use is provided (Form 7.6).

Table 7.4 not only records needs, but also allows you to check all three levels of results. Form 7.5 allows you to (1) identify both current and desired results; (2) has a column for possible means (which are often offered by participants who are confusing ends and means) so that ideas may be entered, but will not be part of the needs assessment; (3) a column to link each need to the mission objective; and (4) the need level to assure coverage of all three levels.

Needs Summary Form

Current Results	Possible Means	Required Results	Existing Mission	Need Level	
				Micro	
				Macro	
				Mega	

Form 7.5. Needs Assessment Summary.

A Needs Assessment Tool Kit—Chapter 7

Form 7.6. Methods-Means Identification Form.

Methods-Means Identification Form

Need Number*	Current Performer SKAAs*	Required Performer SKAAs*	Possible Interventions	**Identify possible ways and means to close the gaps**	
				Cost/Results Analysis	
				Advantages	Disadvantages

*Needs may be clustered...several might deal with some common gaps in results.
** Skills, Knowledges, Attitudes, Abilities.

Form 7.6 provides a methods-means identification form. In each need (or family of needs) current **S**kills, **K**nowledges, **A**ttitudes, and **A**bilities (SKAAs) are compared to required ones so that possible interventions (means, methods) may be identified. A final step (shown as the final column) requires the listing of advantages and disadvantages of each possible intervention. Filling out such a form allows for an objective identification of ways and means to improve performance and meet selected needs.

A Needs, Opportunities, and Maintenance (NOM) analysis

Isn't Needs Assessment always reactive and after-the-fact? Isn't it usually "too late" by the time we do needs assessments?

Needs Assessment may be reactive, proactive, or both. Let's see.

A Needs, Opportunities, and Maintenance (NOM) analysis. It is often fashionable to criticize all training and organizational development efforts and contributions. Some even assert that everything must be thrown out and we should start over. That's nonsense. While there is much which might be constructively changed, we should be careful to also:

- maintain what is working, and
- identify future opportunities and directions.

While most current attention in conventional needs assessment, planning, training, and organizational development is toward reactive actions for fixing, repairing, modifying, and responding to crises, we also have other possibilities.

Resolving Problems Using Needs Assessment. Reactive responses to problems are vital when things are going wrong. Most organizations have plenty of problems which demand immediate attention: low productivity, poor sales, improperly certified technicians, drug use in the workplace, low motivation. Where there are problems, both surfaced and hidden, a needs assessment is important to identify the gaps in results, place them in priority order, and select the most important for resolution.

Needs selected for reduction or elimination are defined as "problems." No gap in results, no need. No need, no problem.

Maintaining What's Working. Not everything in your organization has to be changed. There are many things going on which should be maintained. Much of what is going on and being produced should be preserved by design, not modified while sweeping changes are being made to resolve other problems. Rather than changing what's working—if it "ain't broke don't fix it"—the areas where there are no gaps in performance (needs) should be flagged in order to:

- Make certain that no changes are made to successful means, methods, and resources

and/or

- Develop methods and means to continue what's working so that new needs will not emerge.

Training experiences, for example, might be selected in order to maintain and reinforce existing competencies and abilities. By maintaining their competence, performance will not decline below required levels: performance-related needs will not emerge. If performance and achievement are already at required levels, don't shift what's being done (and how it is being done) unless performance will be improved even more.

Another dimension for maintenance is in the area of continuous improvement of abilities and resources so that needs do not appear. For example, if associates are performing to expected new levels, they might benefit from in-service training in new developments in the field, or in recent policies, products, or methods. Therefore, no new needs will develop.

Opportunity-Finding. In addition to identifying needs and associated problems, there is the proactive task of identifying future requirements (so that future needs will not develop). We also may identify new directions in which to steer. This assessment would identify gaps between What Is and What Could Be.

For example, it is clear that the work place of tomorrow will require substantial information technology abilities (Toffler, 1990). In addition, coop-

A Needs Assessment Tool Kit—Chapter 7

erative work will be in greater demand instead of only using the individual performance skills which are the target of most current training/human resources development practice. Rather than waiting for performance deficits to appear in tomorrow's world (loss in the standard of living through low productivity, drug use, continued disintegration of the family and personal relationships, crime, aggression, etc.), an assessment could seek to identify future requirements, and use those in planning your organization's responses.

An Integrated Approach: NOM Assessment

Because it is vital to identify Needs, Opportunities, and Maintenance requirements, all three perspectives are worth including as part of strategic thinking, planning and needs assessment: a NOM assessments (Kaufman, 1992b). The basic concepts underlying needs assessments still hold: the basic underpinnings are still results and priorities.

A format for a NOM assessment, building on those for needs assessments, could be as shown in Form 7.7.

NOM Assessment Table						
Current Results	Desired Results	Need Exists?		Maintenance Required?		Future Opportunities
		Yes	No	Yes	No	

Form 7.7. A format for a NOM assessment: Needs, Opportunities, Maintenance factors are included. (Based on Kaufman, 1992b.)

By using a NOM assessment, you can add a new dimension to your ability to contribute. It will allow you to add proactive assessment to the usual reactive methods.

How do I know I've covered all the important bases?

Needs Assessment (and Planning) Partnerships

It is important to have representativeness of people—stakeholders—in any needs assessment. Successful needs assessments (as well as strategic planning and total quality management)—and any resulting changes, plans, procedures, and consequences—depend on choosing the correct planning partners to guide and conduct the process. When a representative partnership is formed and the individuals are really included (not asked to be window dressing or rubber stamps) they will more likely "own" the results of the needs assessment when it is completed. An otherwise good needs assessment or related plan might fail merely because uninvolved or unrepresented people may not see that an imposed change, no matter how sensible and rational, might benefit them.

Help assure the adoption of needs assessment results and related plans by the partnership group being carefully selected and all participants actively involved. You may do this by either having affected people participate directly as partners, or by having all groups who will use, do, or receive whatever comes out of the needs assessment, represented in the process. Because of inclusion or representation, all affected will become stakeholders in any resulting plan or recommendations.

The make-up of the planning partnership. There are three human needs assessment and planning partner groups and one performance/data-based one (Kaufman, 1992a, b), as shown in Figures 7.9 and 7.10. The human partners include:

- those who will be affected by the results;
- those who will implement the recommendations; and
- clients or society that will receive (and/or be affected by) the results.

Exactly who should serve as partners depends on the type of organization and who are its clients. Usually the planners and their operational unit (such as personnel, engineering, manufacturing, marketing, quality) will be the implementers and the planners' immediate clients—such as trainees, supervisors, or patients—will be the recipients. "Society" is an inclusive term that encompasses those who will be affected by what an organization and its clients deliver.

For example, in a community service for the differently-abled might include paraplegics, blind, hearing impaired, physically disabled, mentally diminished, ailing and infirm elderly, and their neighbors. Or for an automotive after-market equipment manufacturing, society would include wholesale and retail sales organizations and the end-users. Table 1.2 (page 8) shows the three level of needs assessment: there should be representative partners for each of the three levels. Figure 1.5 (page 12) presented the Organizational Elements Model. Review the various elements, and assure that all five elements are part of the needs assessment team: those concerned with Inputs, Process, Products, Outputs, and Outcomes.

When selecting the planning partners, assure they are typical representatives of their constituencies. If ethnic or age composition is important, obtain a representative sample. If particular skills are critical, be sure that these are represented among the needs assessment partners.

Usually, a stratified random sample—each important partner/stakeholder cluster is represented in terms of how many appear in your organization and its clients—of each partner group will provide representativeness. Don't create large and unwieldy groups—just representative ones.

The number of partners depends on your needs assessment focus and who the planned changes are intended to serve. Because the partner group should represent the actual operational world, it should not include "tokens" nor be packed with friends.

Need: everyone should agree that it refers to a gap in results, not a deficiency in resources or methods. Again, the word **need** has several popular meanings...make sure that all the partners are working with the same (and recommended) definition. The importance of using **need** (as a noun, not a verb) to describe a gap in results cannot be overemphasized.

Needs assessment partners use both hard and soft data in their activities. Both hard and soft data should be used in needs assessment (Figure 7.12). The human partners will supply judgments concerning perceived needs. Because these needs are based on personal observations and feelings, they are termed *needs sensing* or *soft data* because of its attitudinal origins, and because it is not independently verifiable.

Peter Drucker (1973) keeps reminding us that we have to involve all our partners in planning, and in Needs Assessment. Here are some graphics (Figures 7.9 and 7.10) to help you build a planning partnership.

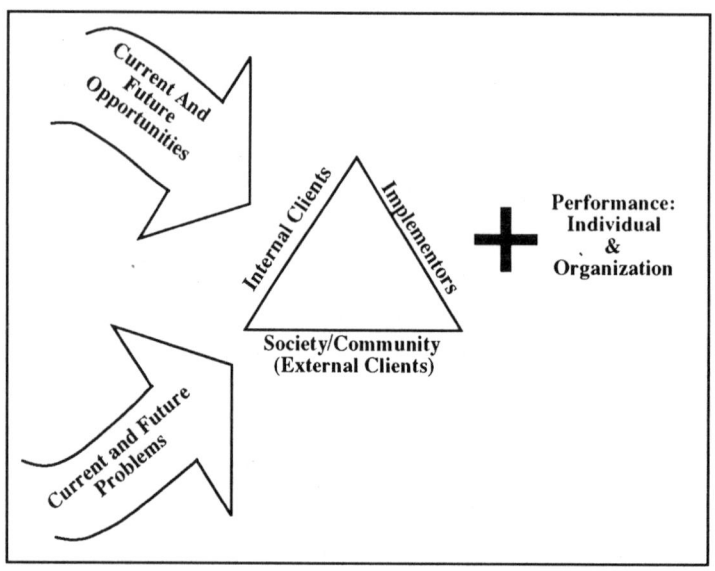

Figure 7.9. The partners (and clients) for planning include employees, managers, and clients/society/community *plus* actual or required performance. Feeding into the partnership are the consideration of current and future opportunities (Kaufman, 1992a).

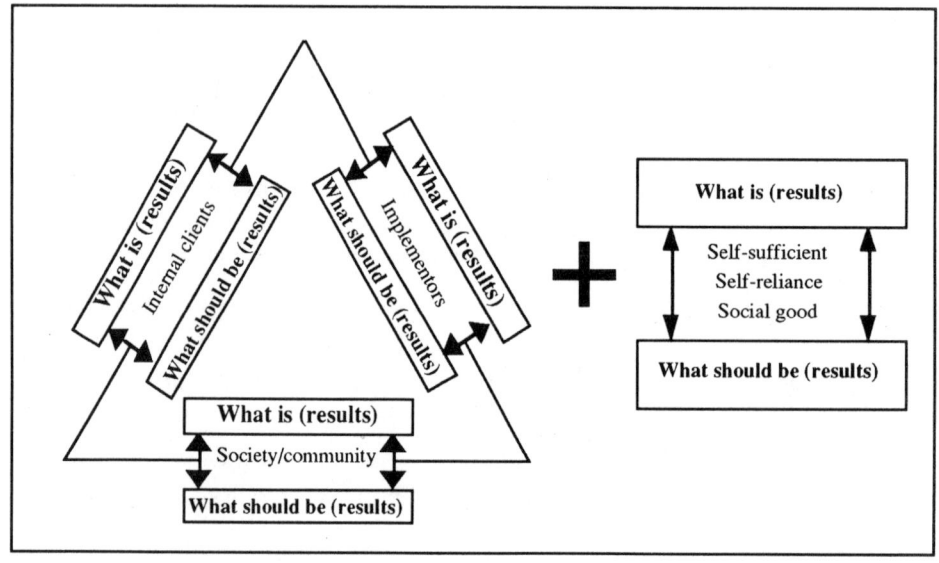

Figure 7.10. The three planning partners—implementors, recipients, and society—provide their perceptions about the gaps in results between what is and what should be (Kaufman, 1992a).

PLANNING PARTNER	WHAT IS	WHAT SHOULD BE
RECIPIENTS (INTERNAL CLIENTS		
IMPLEMENTORS		
SOCIETY (EXTERNAL CLIENTS		

Figure 7.11. Needs Assessment matrix.

We are on more firm ground when we use both hard and soft data. Here, Figure 7.12, is how we merge and cross-check them.

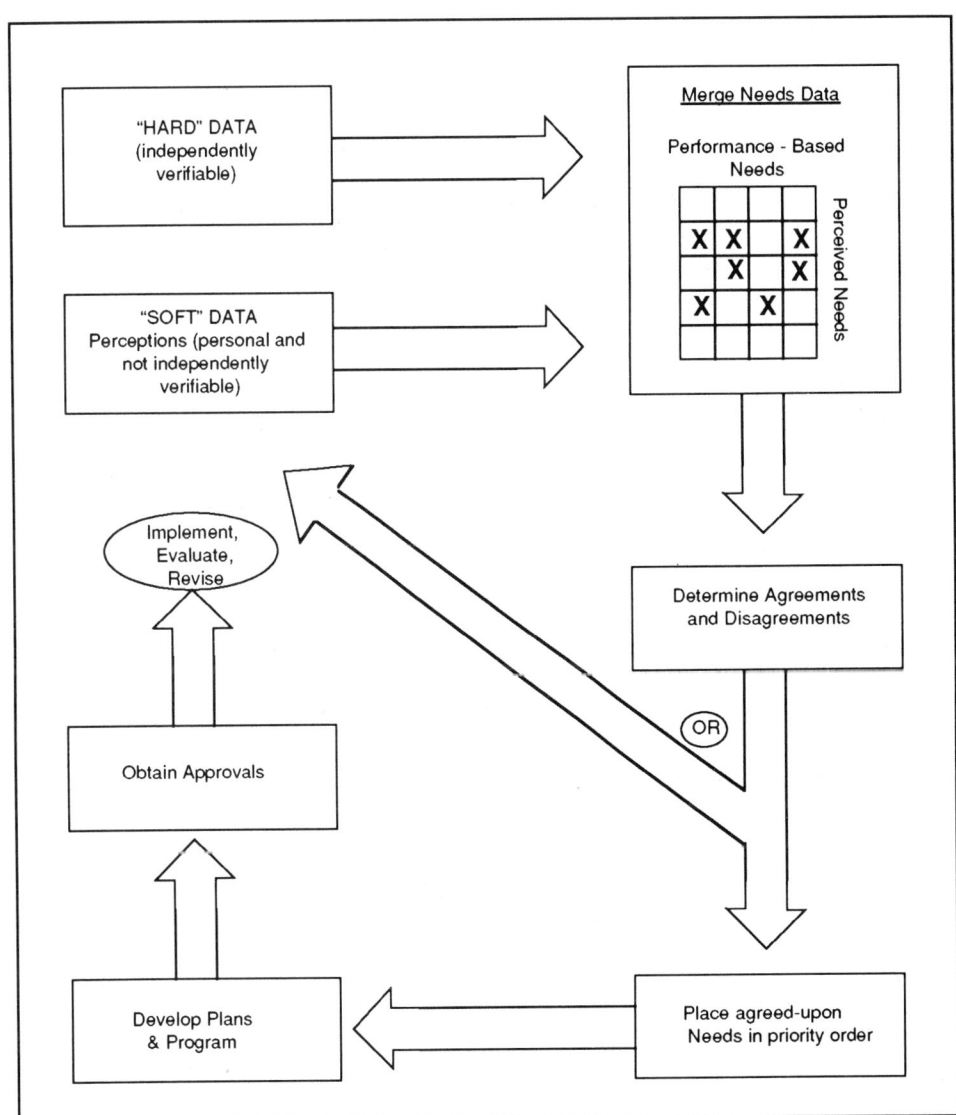

Figure 7.12. A framework for merging hard and soft needs data. Both needs identified through analysis of hard data and soft data should agree before planners move on to planning how to reduce or eliminate them. (Based on Kaufman, 1992a.)

Sensed needs/soft data provide perceived reality and sensitivity to issues of values and preferences about current conditions, problems, opportunities, and consequences. They also may reveal observations concerning the methods and procedures that led to the currently undesired results.

The needs assessment partners will also use data concerning gaps in performance. These independently verifiable needs may be both in human and organizational performance. Such data is termed *hard data* because it derives from actual observed performance, and is independently verifiable. Hard data should be collected at all three levels of results: Mega/outcomes, Macro/outputs, and Micro/products.

Hard data collection and its use frequently gets people out of their comfort zones simply because performance related information raises the specter of blame and fault finding. Assure the partners that performance data is to be used in the needs assessment for improving or fixing, not for blaming. The partnership operates best when free from personal agendas and personal fear.

Performance-based data may be viewed as a nonhuman partner because it supplies additional independently verifiable, unemotional facts the partnership should consider in identifying, documenting, and selecting needs. Together, the sensed needs/soft data which is supplied by the implementers and recipients, and external society/clients plus the performance-based data provides the core information for a useful and valid needs assessment.

The partnership must feel comfortable with (a) a results orientation, (b) the definition of need as a noun, not a verb, and (c) the importance of utilizing both hard and soft data. In order to have a common destination to guide them, a Mega-level ideal vision will serve the partnership well.

Obtaining the planning partners' participation. It isn't enough to only identify the needs assessment partners. They must become active participants and contributors as well. Contact the selected partners and declare to each the expectations, required time commitments, desired products, and level of contributions. Disclose how much you will support them: with funds, travel, data, materials, support services, and the like. Be clear concerning how the organization will use and apply their the results and recommendations from the needs assessment.

After getting commitments from the partners, design and schedule the first and subsequent meetings. Meetings can be face-to-face or round table affairs or can include written surveys, delphi techniques, teleconferencing, or computer/E-mail interfaces. Replace partners who don't come, have a single-issue agenda, or don't contribute.

Obtaining acceptance of the needs assessment and planning level. Share with the partners the three needs assessment and planning levels—Mega, Macro, and Micro. Get their commitment to the level, ideally (and practically) Mega. By familiarizing them with the optional levels and the advantages and disadvantages of each, you allow the partners an informed choice. It is important that all partners know the scope of the needs assessment and have a common set of understandings and expectations. This common frame of reference beginning is critical, and as much time as necessary should be committed to obtaining this understanding and acceptance.

Explain the basic concepts of needs assessment to the partners. Share with them that needs assessment is the process for identifying, documenting, and justifying the gaps between "what is" and "what should be" concerning the three types of results identified in Table 1.4 and Figure 7.11: Outcomes/Mega, Outputs/Macro, and Products/Micro. Inform them they will have to decide which gaps to close first. Have them agree that there may be (and should be) three levels of needs assessments—one relating to each of the three types of results. The open arrows shown in Figure 1.6 (page 13) identifies possible needs assessments, and the cross-hatched arrows are possible Quasi Needs Assessments. The Mega level of needs assessment is strongly recommended.

Common understandings are critical to valid results: Needs analysis, although some might initially think so, is different from needs assessment and from front-end analysis. Remember that the needs assessment team will come into the partnership with different understandings, experiences, and beliefs about needs assessment. One frequent misunderstanding is that needs assessment, needs analysis, and front end analysis are all the same. They are not, and you can help the partnership by explaining what each is and how each may make an important contribution to organizational and human performance improvement.

Needs analysis (Kaufman & Valentine, 1989) consists of determining the gaps between adjacent organizational elements (refer to Figure 1.5), and finding the causes of the inability for one level (e.g., products, when aggregated), to deliver required results at the next, e.g., outputs, and/or those in turn delivering outcomes. *Front-end analysis* is a general term for any analysis which comes before selecting solutions and resources. Usually, front-end analysis starts at the Macro/Outputs or the Micro/Products level: after all, in order to analyze a need, you have to identify and select it (a product of needs assessment) first.

While it is tempting to slide over differences among needs assessment partners in terms of the words they use, and the concepts the employ, it will be punishing not to have everyone on the same needs assessment team. A common destination and shared concepts are vital to an effective partnership.

Trust is an essential ingredient of any needs assessment partnership. If any interpersonal breakdowns occur, coolly straighten out any misunderstandings. The partnership must function as a team, and work together with trust and mutual respect and shared purposes.

Needs Assessment checklist

Following (on the next page) is a checklist with aids to help you cover your bases. Table 7.5 provides guidance on relating some major considerations to many of the tools presented in this chapter.

	Check	Yes	No	If no, use or complete	More info? Read
1.	Will the needs assessment answer the key and critical questions which any organization must ask and answer?			Table 7.1, 7.2 Figure 7.2	Chapter 1
2.	Does the needs assessment focus on ends and not means?			Form 7.4, 7.8 Figure 7.1 Table 7.4	Chapter 1 and 5
3.	Do you focus on gaps in results, not gaps or lacks in resources or processes?			Form 7.4, 7.5	Chapter 1 and 5
4.	Do you avoid using need as a verb, (e.g., "What do you need."), and thus avoid accidentally shifting the focus to means and resources?			Form 7.6, 7.8 Figure 7.1	Chapter 1 and 5
5.	Do you relate and align the three levels of need assessment Mega (outcome-level of results), Macro (output-level of results), Micro (product-level of results)?			Table 7.3, 7.4 Figure 7.1, 7.2, 7.6, 7.7, 7.8 Form 7.4, 7.8	Chapter 1 and 6
6.	Will the assessment address the needs, opportunities, and maintenance (continuing what is working)? Does it deal with more than problems?			Form 7.7	Chapter 7
7.	Have you included both "hard" (independently verifiable) and "soft" (personal, private, perceptions) data in your needs assessment?			Form 7.8, 7.12	Chapter 2, 3, 4, and 5
8.	Are the results (performance, accomplishment, consequences) data collected for all three levels of need assessment?			Form 7.1, 7.2, 7.3, 7.4, 7.8 Figure 7.1, 7.2, 7.6 Table 7.4, 7.4	Chapter 1 and 6
9.	Are the data valid and reliable?			Table 7.5	Chapter 7
10.	Have you identified and involved all "key" partners, including recipients, implementors, and society and/or community?			Form 7.7, Figure 7.9, 7.10, 7.11	Chapter 1 and 2
11.	Have you related Needs Assessment with Needs Analysis Design, and implementation?			Figure 7.3	Chapter 1 and 6
12.	Do you have a systematic process for assessing needs?			Form 7.8 Figure 7.4, 7.5, 7.6	Chapter 7

Table 7.5. Matching some Needs Assessment questions to the material in this book.

When you develop a questionnaire for a Needs Assessment, use Form 7.8 as a checklist to help.

THINGS TO CONSIDER IN DEVELOPING A NEEDS ASSESSMENT QUESTIONNAIRE, AND COLLECTING DATA

_____ 1. Make certain that the questions are about results, not about processes or inputs.

_____ 2. Ask about perceptions of gaps in results for both dimensions–*what is* and *what should be*.

_____ 3. Ask about the three levels of needs:
- External.
- Organizational contributions.
- Building-block results (products).

_____ 4. Assure validity and reliability.

_____ 5. Make the questionnaire long enough to get reliable responses, but short enough that people will actually respond.

_____ 6. Use an approach that makes it clear to respondents exactly what is wanted. People usually don't want to write long answers, so a checklist will reduce their burden while making the questionnaire easier to score.

_____ 7. Don't ask questions that reveal, directly or indirectly, a bias. Don't use the data-collection vehicle to set up the responses you really want.

_____ 8. Ask several questions about each dimension or issue. Ask about each concern in different ways, to assure reliability in the responses. Basing any decision on answers to one question is risky.

_____ 9. Try the data-collection instrument on a sample group to identify problems in meaning, coverage, and scorability. Revise it as required.

When collecting performance (or "hard") data:

_____ 10. Make certain the data collected relates to important issues for which you want answers.

_____ 11. Assure yourself that the data you use are collected correctly and that the methods used for gathering it and reporting it are free from bias.

_____ 12. Assure yourself that the data are based upon enough observations to make them reliable, not a one-shot happening.

_____ 13. Make certain that the data can be independently verified and cross-checked.

Form 7.8. A checklist to use when developing a questionnaire (Kaufman, 1992a, with permission).

Application Exercise

Identifying Needs statements at various levels discussed in this book.

And just to refresh yourself, try this self-assessment.

A list of statements follow. Indicate the correct needs assessment level (i.e., Mega, Macro, Micro, or Quasi) by writing it in the space provided.

1. The Region III Collections current at the annual level of $15.8 million should be raised to at least $19.5 million during the following fiscal year to meet the projected budget goal.

    The $19.5 million would be considered_____.

2. Within 6 months of graduation and placement effort, at least 90 percent of all graduates of Automotive Vocational Training Programs of our school will get and keep an auto-mechanics job at a salary above the minimum wage and not receive government support.

    The 90% completers keeping a job at minimum wage and without government support would be considered_____.

3. To implement mental health residential treatment programs to serve Martin, Oakland, Indian River, and San Francisco County residents by the end of the coming fiscal year.

    Implementing the programs would be considered_____.

4. To complete pre-service training and certification of competence for all new employees and incumbents with less than one year's tenure in all Sales and Customer Service positions in the international division within 180 days of the date of employment for new employees and by December 31 of the next year for all incumbents with less than one year's tenure.

    The completed training would be considered_____.

5. The number of customer complaints received in Customer Services should be reduced by 50% as compared with last quarter's complaints to achieve the Department objective by the following two quarters.

   The reduced number of complaints would be considered _____.

6. The average length of successful (meeting all placement success criteria) placement in shelter care of dependent juveniles is now 28 days due to treatment effectiveness problems. It should be 25 days (or less) by the end of next summer semester to comply with court order.

   The reduced average length of successful placements would be considered_____.

7. To increase at least by 50 percent the number of car loan applications in Branch Cupertino, from 26 to 39 by the end of the second quarter of the current fiscal year.

   To increase at least 50 percent the number of car loan applications would be considered_____.

8. The Manufacturing Department at Mountain View had no employee recognition program during the last fiscal year. A program will be developed and implemented by the next fiscal year.

   The development and implementation of the employee recognition program would be considered_____.

9. The overall statewide average civil discharge rate to state mental health hospitals exceeded 50 persons per 100,000 total population during the last fiscal year. The rate will have to exceed 40 persons per 100,000 total population during the next fiscal year to achieve the goal of deinstitutionalization.

   To decrease the overall statewide civil discharge rate would be considered_____.

10. We "need" more training in total quality management.

The need for more training would be considered_____.

Compare your answers to the following

- Statements 2 and 5 are examples of **Needs at Mega level**. These statements express the effects that the *Organizational Results—Outcomes*, have on society—see Chapter 2.

- Statements 6 and 9 are examples of **Needs at Macro level**. These statements indicate the *(Organizational Results—Outputs)* produced that will effectively impact society when delivered—see Chapter 3.

- Statements 1 and 4 are examples of **Needs at Micro level**. These statements indicate the *Organizational Results—Products)* produced that will effectively impact society when delivered—see Chapter 4.

- Statements 3, 7, 8, and 10 are examples of **Quasi Needs**. They describe the resources and means *(Organizational Efforts)* required by the organization or individual to produce results—see Chapter 5.

A Final Suggestion

Above all, empower yourself to shift old paradigms in order to deliver true quality—results which are useful to all. This book will help you assess needs, a vital part of achieving useful results as payoffs.

References and Suggested Readings

Drucker, P. F. (1973) *Management: Tasks, responsibilities, practices.* New York: Harper & Row.

Kaufman, R. (1992a) *Strategic planning plus: An organizational guide.* Newbury Park, CA: Sage Publishing.

Kaufman, R. (1992b) *Mapping educational success.* Newbury Park, Ca: Corwin Press, Division of Sage.

Kaufman, R. & Valentine, G. (1989, Nov.) Relating needs assessment and needs analysis. *Performance & Instruction.*

Toffler, N. (1990) *Powershift: Knowledge, wealth, and balance at the edge of the 21st century.* New York: Bantam

Bibliography

Bennis, W. & Nannus, B. (1985) *Leaders: The strategies for taking charge.* New York: Harper & Row.

Bhote, K. R. (1989, Autumn) The Malcolm Baldridge Quality Award. *National Productivity Review,* Vol. 8, No. 4.

Carlisle, K. E. (1986) *Analyzing jobs and tasks.* Englewood Cliffs, NJ: Educational Technology Publications.

Crosby, P. B. (1986) *Quality without tears: The art of hassle-free management.* New York: New American Library.

Deal, T. F. (1991) *Developing a quality culture.* In R. H. Kilmann, I. Kilmann, & Associates. *Making organizations competitive: Enhancing networks and relationships across traditional boundaries.* San Francisco: Jossey-Bass.

DeYoung, H. G. (1990, Feb. 19) Tiny resistor maker keeps its eyes on the Baldridge prize. *Electronic Business.*

Drucker, P. F. (1973) *Management: Tasks, responsibilities, practices.* New York: Harper & Row.

Drucker, P. F. (1992, Sept.-Oct.) The new society of organizations. *Harvard Business Review.*

Gilbert, T. F. (1978) *Human competence: Engineering worthy performance.* New York: McGraw-Hill.

Gilbert, T. F. & Gilbert, M. B. (1989, Jan.) Performance engineering: Making human productivity a science. *Performance and Instruction.*

Harless, J. H. (1975) *An ounce of analysis is worth a pound of cure.* Newnan, GA: Harless Performance Guild.

Kanter, R. M. (1989) *When giants learn to dance: Mastering the challenges of strategy, management, and careers in the 1990s.* New York: Simon & Schuster.

Kaufman, R. (1987, Oct.) A needs assessment primer. *Training & Development Journal.*

Kaufman, R. (1988, Sept.) Preparing useful performance indicators. *Training & Development Journal.*

Kaufman, R. (1989, Feb.) Who is the client? Who benefits? *Performance & Instruction.*

Kaufman, R. (1991, Dec.) Toward total quality "plus." *Training,* Vol. 28, No. 12.

Kaufman, R. (1990, June) Performance technology and quality management: Conflict or new partnership? *Educational Technology.*

Kaufman, R. (1988) *Planning educational systems: A results-based approach.* Lancaster, PA: Technomic Publishing.

Kaufman, R. (1992a) *Strategic planning plus: An organizational guide.* Newbury Park, CA: Sage Publishing.

Kaufman, R. (1992b) *Mapping educational success.* Newbury Park, CA: Corwin Press, Division of Sage.

Kaufman, R. & Herman, J. (1991) *Strategic planning in education: Rethinking, restructuring, revitalizing.* Lancaster, PA: Technomic Publishing.

Kaufman, R. & Rojas, A. (1985) *Needs assessment.* Tallahassee, FL: Florida State Department of Health and Rehabilitative Services and the Center for Needs Assessment and Planning.

Kaufman, R., Stith, S., & Kaufman, J. (1992, Feb.) Extending performance technology to improve strategic market planning. *Performance and Instruction.*

Kaufman, R. & Thiagarajan, S. (1987) Identifying and specifying requirements for instruction. In R. M. Gagné (Ed.), *Instructional technology: Foundations.* Hillsdale, NJ: Lawrence Erlbaum Associates.

Kaufman, R. & Valentine, G. (1989, Nov.) Relating needs assessment and needs analysis. *Performance & Instruction.*

Mager, R. F. (1975) *Preparing instructional objectives* (2nd Ed.). Belmont, CA: David S. Lake Publishers.

Mager, R. F. & Pipe, P. (1984) *Analyzing performance problems* (2nd Ed.). Belmont, CA: Pitman.

Mayer H. & Coldeway, D.O. (1990) *TIP-research report #1: Training and performance improvement: Needs in business and industry.* Athabasca, Alberta: Athabasca University.

Ohmae, K. (1982) *The mind of the strategist: Business planning for competitive advantage.* New York: Penguin Books.

Pascale, R. T. & Athos, A. G. (1981) *The art of Japanese management: Applications for American executives.* New York: Warner.

Peters, T. (1987) *Thriving on chaos: Handbook for a management revolution.* New York: Alfred A. Knopf.

Pfeiffer, J. W., Goodstein, L. D., & Nolan, T. M. (1989) *Shaping strategic planning: Frogs, bees, and turkey tails.* Glenview, IL: Scott, Foresman & Co.

Rojas, A. & Mulkey, J. (1991, June) Have the cake and eat it too: Theory applied to the real world. *Performance & Instruction.*

Rossett, A. (1987) *Training needs assessment.* Englewood Cliffs, NJ: Educational Technology Publications.

Rummler, G. A. & Brache, A. P. (1990) *Improving performance: How to manage the white space on the organization chart.* San Francisco, CA: Jossey-Bass.

Senge, P. M. (1990) *The fifth discipline: The art & practice of the learning organization.* New York: Doubleday.

Toffler, N. (1990) *Powershift: Knowledge, wealth, and balance at the edge of the 21st century.* New York: Bantam.

Wolfe, P. *et al.* (1991) *Job-task analysis: Guide to good practice.* Englewood Cliffs, NJ: Educational Technology Publications.

Index

B

Baldridge Award, 57-58
Bennis, W., 56
Bhote, K. R., 58
Brache, A. P., 87, 103
Building-block objectives
 defined, 40
 guidelines for setting, 41-42
 purposes served by, 40-41

C

Client-centered actions, characteristic of Macro-level needs assessment, 56
Client concurrence
 importance of, 42, 69, 91-92
 with Macro-level needs, 69-70
 with Mega-level needs, 42-43
 with Micro-level needs, 91-92
Client satisfaction, 58
Constraints, identifying and eliminating, 115-116
Crosby, P. B., 57
Current status of organizational output
 determining, 63-65
 sources for information about, 64
Current status of vision variables
 data needed to determine, 34-35
 determining, 33-36
 guidelines for determining, 35-36
 prioritizing needs in Mega-level gaps between current status and ideal vision, 36-38

D

Data. *See* Hard data; Soft data
Data collecting steps in strategic planning, 129, 132
Data collection checklists, 154-158
Data sources
 for Macro-level needs assessment, 63, 64
 for Mega-level needs assessment, 34-35
 for Micro-level needs assessment, 83, 84
 for Quasi needs assessment, 107, 108-109
Deal, T. F., 57

Deming Award, 57-58
DeYoung, H. G., 57
Drucker, Peter, 18, 170

E

Ends and means, importance of distinction between, 4
External/societal contribution of organizations, 7

F

Front-end analysis, 174

H

Hard data
 for Macro-level needs assessment, 62
 for Mega-level needs assessment, 34
 for Micro-level needs assessment, 82-83
 performance-based data, 172
 for Quasi needs assessment, 108
 used by needs assessment and planning partnerships, 169, 171-172
Herman, J., 41

I

Ideal vision
 aligning Macro-level needs with, 66-67
 aligning Micro-level needs with, 87
 as basis for needs assessment and planning, 28
 creating, 31-33
 data needed for determining current status of, 34-35
 defining vision for, 28-29
 determining current status of, 33-36
 determining, for an organization, 28-33
 importance of, 30-31
 prioritizing needs in Mega-level gaps between current status and ideal vision, 36-38

in public and private sectors,
29-30
Implementation and evaluation step
in strategic planning, 131,
132
Inputs, for Organizational Elements
Model (OEM), 11-12
Internal products of organizations,
7

K

Kanter, R. M., 56
Kaufman, J., 57
Kaufman, R., 6, 7, 11, 13, 25, 31,
25, 31, 41, 53, 56, 57, 58,
59, 59, 60, 61, 102, 115,
117, 127, 129, 131, 132, 152,
159, 160, 167, 168, 169, 170,
174, 176

M

Macro-level needs, 65-66
listing alternative methods and
means for addressing, 70
presenting to clients for
concurrence, 69-70
prioritizing, 67-68
Macro-level needs assessment
See also Needs assessment
aligning needs with ideal vision
and mission of organization,
66-67
checklist for recording data
collection, 156
client-centered actions
characteristic of, 56
defined, 53-54
determining current quality of
organizational output, 63-65
determining desired quality of
organizational output, 61-63
listing alternative methods and
means for addressing Macro-
level needs, 70
listing identified, agreed upon
needs, 65-66
occasions for use of, 55-57
presenting Macro-level needs to
clients for concurrence,
69-70
prioritizing Macro-level needs,
67-68
steps in, 16, 61-70
Macro-level organizational
effectiveness, 125
Macro-level strategic planning, 128
Market-driven approaches, 56-57,
133
proactive, 57
reactive, 57
Means and ends, importance of
distinction between, 4
Mega-level needs
identifying and listing
alternative methods for
addressing, 43-44
presenting to clients for
concurrence, 42-43
prioritizing, 36-38
Mega-level needs assessment
also Ideal vision; Needs
assessment
breaking down mission objective
to building-block objectives,
40-42
checklist for recording data
collection, 155
defined, 25-26
determining ideal vision step in,
28-33
determining current status of
variables in vision
statement, 33-36
flow chart showing functions to
complete, 151
identifying and listing methods
and means for addressing
Mega-level needs, 43-44
occasions for use of, 27
presenting needs to clients for
concurrence, 42-43
prioritizing needs in gap between
current status and ideal
vision, 36-38
process of, 26
questions to encourage client
participation, 144-146
steps in, 14, 27-44
writing mission objectives for,
38-39
Mega-level organizational
effectiveness, 125
Mega-level strategic planning, 128
Micro-level needs
aligning with ideal vision and
organizational mission, 87
identifying and listing
alternative methods and means
of addressing, 92-93
listing identified, agreed upon

needs, 85-86
presenting to clients for
concurrence, 91-92
prioritizing, 87-91
Micro-level needs assessment
See also Needs assessment
checklist for recording data
collection, 157
defined, 80
determining current performance,
84-85
determining required performance
in terms of measurable
accomplishments, 82-83
identifying and listing
alternative methods and means
of addressing Micro-level
needs, 92-93
listing gaps in performance,
85-86
listing identified, agreed upon
Micro-level needs, 85-86
presenting Micro-level needs to
clients for concurrence,
91-92
prioritizing Micro-level needs,
87-91
steps in, 16, 82-93
when and why to use, 81-82
Micro-level organizational
effectiveness, 125
Micro-level strategic planning, 128
Mission objectives
defined, 38
writing, 38-39
Mission statement
aligning Macro-level needs with,
66-67
aligning Micro-level needs with,
87

N

Nannus, B., 56
Needs
ends/means distinction applied
to, 4
identified as gaps in results,
consequences, or
accomplishments, 4-5
Needs, Opportunities, and
Maintenance (NOM) analysis,
165-167
Needs analysis, 102-103, 174
Needs assessment
See also Macro-level needs
assessment; Mega-level needs
assessment; Micro-level needs
assessment; Quasi needs
assessment
algorithm for dealing with
assigned problems, 152-153
algorithm to assure linkage
between levels, 160
algorithm to determine linkage
between levels, 159
application exercise for, 177-179
checklists for, 174-176
convincing clients of need for,
142
determining scope and procedures,
146, 148-153
form to determine questions to
pursue, 148
frameworks for, 9, 10
functions of, 5
guide for, 149
guide for relating needs to gaps
in results, 143
ideal vision as basis for, 28
identifying methods and means for
eliminating or reducing gaps,
162, 164-165
levels of, 8-9. *See also* Macro-
level needs assessment; Mega-
level needs assessment;
Micro-level needs assessment
levels of, identifying, 154
levels of, questions to ask when
selecting, 147
levels of, relationships among,
9, 104
levels of, relationships among
forming chain of results,
127-128
maintaining what's working, 166
marketing, 142-146
Needs, Opportunities, and
Maintenance (NOM) analysis,
165-167
objectives for, 142-144
occasions for use of, 3
opportunity-finding, 166-167
Organizational Elements Model
(OEM) as framework for,
11-14, 126-127
partnership with planning
essential for, 17-18
proactive approach recommended,
57
procedures outlined, 2
purpose of, 3

recommended steps for, 14-15
relating to organizational
  effectiveness and strategic
  planning, 125-126
relationship of Organizational
  Elements Model (OEM) to, 13
relationship with strategic
  planning, 128-129
resolving problems using, 165-166
role and function in strategic
  planning and organizational
  effectiveness, 131
sequence of generic steps for,
  150
strategic thinking essential to,
  134
and Total Quality Management
  (TQM), 57-59
and Total Quality Management
  Plus, 59-61
Needs assessment and planning
  partnerships, 168-174
agreement on definition of need,
  169
common understandings critical to
  valid results, 173-174
data used by, 169, 171, 171-172
make-up of planning partnership,
  168-169, 170
obtaining acceptance of levels
  for needs assessment and
  planning, 173
obtaining partners'
  participation, 172-173
Needs assessment and strategic
  planning agreement table, 145
Needs sensing. *See* Soft data
Needs summary, 162

O

Organizational effectiveness
improving, 134-137
integrated rolling-down/rolling-
  up approach to improving, 137
at the Macro level, 125
at the Mega level, 125
at the Micro level, 125
questions to be asked before
  selecting needs assessment
  level, 126
reactive and proactive planning
  in, 133
relating to needs assessment and
  strategic planning, 125-126
role and function of needs
  assessment in, 131
rolling-down approach to
  improving, 136
rolling-up approach to improving,
  134-135
Organizational Elements Model (OEM)
elements of, 11-13
relating level/scope of planning
  and needs assessment, clients
  and beneficiaries, and
  results, 12, 126-127
relationship to needs assessment,
  13
Organizational mission
aligning Macro-level needs with,
  66-67
aligning Micro-level needs with,
  87
Organizational output
determining current quality of,
  63-65
determining desired quality of,
  61-63
Organizational resources,
  processes, products, and
  contributions, aligning with
  societal consequences, 161
Organizational resources and
  methods
determining current availability
  and/or quality of, 108-109
determining desired availability
  and/or quality of, 105, 107
determining gaps between desired
  and current status (Quasi
  needs), 109-111
Organizational vision. *See* Ideal
  vision
Organization outputs, 7
Organizations
determining ideal vision for,
  28-33. *See also* Ideal
  vision
external/societal contribution
  of, 7
internal products of, 7
levels of results in, 7
outputs from, 7
questions to be asked about, 6
Outcomes, from Organizational
  Elements Model (OEM), 11-12,
  127
Outputs
from Organizational Elements
  Model (OEM), 12, 127
organization outputs, 7

P

Performance
See also Micro-level needs assessment
  determining current performance, 84-85
  determining required performance in terms of measurable accomplishments, 82-83
  listing gaps in, 85-86
Performance-based data, 172
Peters, T., 56
Planning
See also Needs assessment and planning partnerships; Strategic planning
  ideal vision as basis for, 28
  partnership with needs assessment essential, 17-18
  reactive and proactive, 133
  level/scope of, in Organizational Elements Model (OEM), 12
Planning steps in strategic planning, 129, 131, 132
Proactive market-driven approaches, 57
Proactive planning, 133
Processes, in Organizational Elements Model (OEM), 12, 127
Products
  from Organizational Elements Model (OEM), 12-13, 127
  internal products, 7

Q

Quality of life, and determining organization's current status regarding vision statement, 33-36
Quasi needs
  aligning with needs identified at Micro, Macro, and Mega levels, 111
  determining, 109-111
  identify alternative methods and means for addressing, 113-114
  identifying advantages and disadvantages of alternative methods and means, 114-115
  prioritizing based on cost to ignore vs. cost to address, 111-113
Quasi needs assessment, 9
  aligning Quasi needs with needs identified at Micro, Macro, and Mega levels, 111
  checklist for recording data collection, 158
  defined, 9, 101-102
  determining Quasi needs, 109-111
  guidelines for eliminating constraints, 116
  identify alternative methods and means for addressing Quasi needs, 113-114
  identifying advantages and disadvantages of alternative methods and means of addressing Quasi needs, 114-115
  identifying constraints, 115-116
  occasions for use of, 11
  place Quasi needs in order of importance based on cost to address vs. cost to ignore, 111-113
  presenting alternative means and methods to clients, 116-117
  specifying desired availability and/or quality of organizational resources and methods, 105, 107
  steps in, 17, 105-117
  steps summarized, 106
  when and why to perform, 102-105

R

Reactive market-driven approaches, 57
Reactive planning, 133
Results
  levels of, 7
  needs as gaps in, 4-5
Rolled-up elements in total quality management programs, 59-61
Rolling-down approach to needs assessment and planning, 136
Rolling-down/rolling-up integrated approach to needs assessment and planning, 137
Rolling-up approach to needs assessment and planning, 134-135
Rossett, A., 103
Rummler, G. A., 87, 103
Scoping step in strategic planning, 129
Sensed needs. *See* Soft data

S

Societal consequences
 aligning organizational resources, processes, products, and contributions with, 161
 questions to be asked about, 6, 7
Soft data
 for Macro-level needs assessment, 62
 for Mega-level needs assessment, 34
 for Micro-level needs assessment, 83
 for Quasi needs assessment, 108
 used by needs assessment and planning partnerships, 169, 171-172
Stith, M., 57
Strategic planning
 See also Planning
 data collection steps for, 129
 framework summarized, 132
 implementation step for, 131
 levels to initiate, 128-129
 at the Macro and Micro level, 128
 Mega-holistic framework for, 129-132
 planning steps for, 129, 131
 relating to needs assessment and organizational effectiveness, 125-126
 relationship with needs assessment, 128-129
 role and function of needs assessment in, 131
 scoping steps for, 129
 strategic thinking essential to, 134
 twelve step process for, 129, 131
Strategic planning plus, 31, 131
Strategic thinking, 134

T

Toffler, N., 166
Total quality awards, 57-58
Total Quality Management (TQM), 53
 and needs assessment, 57-58
Total Quality Management (TQM) program, linked (rolled-up) elements in, 59
Total Quality Management Plus, and needs assessment, 59-61
Total quality management plus program, linked (rolled-up) elements in, 59-61
Total quality programs
 elements rolling-up in, 58
 rolling-down and rolling-up sequences of elements in, 60
Training needs assessment, drawbacks of, 103

V

Valentine, G., 102, 174